CASE STUDIES IN

CULTURAL ANTHROPOLOGY

GENERAL EDITORS

George and Louise Spindler

STANFORD UNIVERSITY

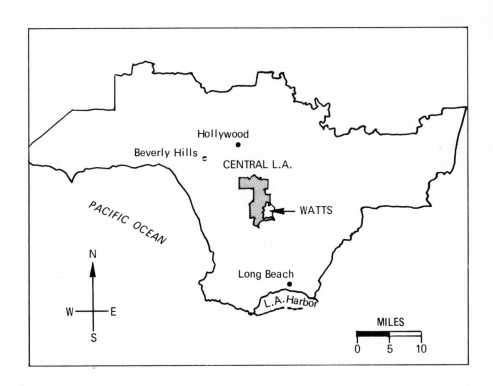

Hollywood

Beverly Hills

CENTRAL L.A.

WATTS

PACIFIC OCEAN

N

W — E

S

Long Beach

L.A. Harbor

MILES

0   5   10

WATTS AND WOODSTOCK

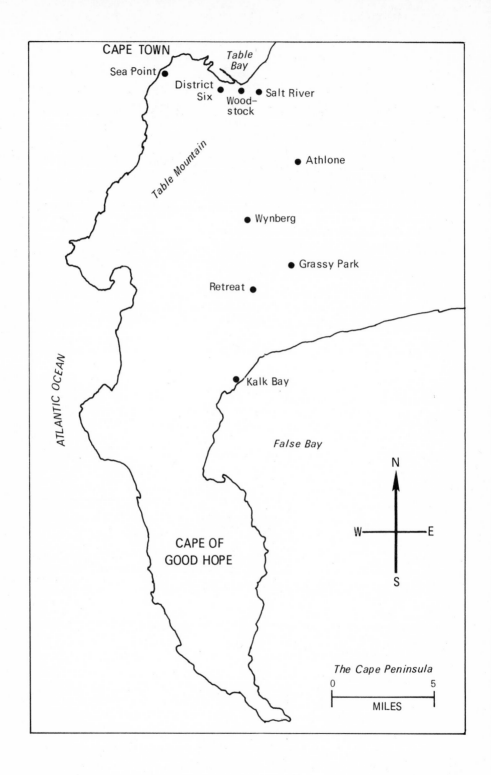

CAPE TOWN

Sea Point

District
Six

Wood-
stock

Salt River

*Table
Bay*

Table Mountain

Athlone

Wynberg

Grassy Park

Retreat

ATLANTIC OCEAN

Kalk Bay

False Bay

CAPE OF
GOOD HOPE

N

W   E

S

The Cape Peninsula

0   5

MILES

WATTS AND WOODSTOCK

Identity and Culture
in the United States and South Africa

By

JAMES O'TOOLE

HOLT, RINEHART AND WINSTON

NEW YORK   CHICAGO   SAN FRANCISCO   ATLANTA
DALLAS   MONTREAL   TORONTO   LONDON   SYDNEY

Cover: Watts Towers; Coon Troupe in Woodstock

Library of Congress Catalog Card Number: 72–85483
ISBN: 0–03–0009367
Printed in the United States of America
3 4 5 6 7   059   1 2 3 4 5 6 7 8 9

Foreword

About the Series

These case studies in cultural anthropology are designed to bring to students, in beginning and intermediate courses in the social sciences, insights into the richness and complexity of human life as it is lived in different ways and in different places. They are written by men and women who have lived in the societies they write about and who are professionally trained as observers and interpreters of human behavior. Most of the authors are also teachers, and in writing their books they have kept the students who will read them foremost in their minds. It is our belief that when an understanding of ways of life very different from one's own is gained, abstractions and generalizations about social structure, cultural values, subsistence techniques, and the other universal categories of human social behavior become meaningful.

About the Author

James O'Toole received his doctorate in social anthropology in 1970 from Oxford University, where he was a Rhodes Scholar. While an undergraduate at the University of Southern California, he founded and for three years was a director of a tutorial project for black children from the Los Angeles ghetto. In Africa for most of 1968, he studied the social consequences of racial and ethnic conflict in South Africa, particularly as it compared to the American experience. He has worked as a journalist, a management consultant, and as Director of Field Research for the President's Commission on Campus Unrest, and as a Special Assistant to the Secretary, Department of Health, Education and Welfare. Currently, he is the chairman of the Secretary's Committee on Work in America.

About the Book

This is a compelling, disturbing, yet hopeful case study of two communities in which racial minorities struggle against the overwhelming social constraints imposed upon them by powerful, dominant groups. Woodstock is a part of the Cape Coloured quarter of Cape Town, in the Republic of South Africa. Watts is in the black ghetto of Los Angeles, California.

The Coloured people of Woodstock are subjected to the racial system of *apartheid* (pronounced apart-hate) that is similar to the Jim Crow legislation that existed until recently in the Southern United States. The parallels between the effects of *apartheid* on the lives of the Coloured people, and the effects of past and present discrimination against the black citizens of Watts, are significant and unsettling. Although in South Africa inequities in educational and economic opportunity and discrimination in housing and social matters are the requirements of law, for black Americans the results of customary and illegal discrimination are often as deep and as painful. For example, the denial of access to political power has historically been almost as severe in Watts as in Woodstock. And, in both communities, there is a self-defeating dependency upon white society, white largesse, white norms, and white goals. The consequences in both instances are the loss of self-respect and the absence of a meaningful and rewarding personal identity. Dr. O'Toole makes such similarities between Watts and Woodstock abundantly clear without labeling them all explicitly.

But there is a difference between Watts and Woodstock, and a hopeful one at least for the people of Watts—and for America in general. After the Watts riots in the summer of 1965 important changes began to appear in the community. Strivings for identity, recognition, power, and pride began to emerge from a previously demoralized people. That some forms of this new black expression frighten some members of the white and black communities is not surprising. But it seems undeniable that within this movement ultimately lies hope for positive change. As the movement within the black community occurs, white society also changes. This demonstrates that however separate blacks may become in their struggle for identity, in the final analysis, blacks and whites, as parts of American society, are interdependent. This important fact is overlooked in South Africa where the official policy reflects an attempt to dismantle what is, in reality, a whole. This policy is, of course, a chimera. America can learn, therefore, from the South African experience that failure to provide equal opportunity and justice to all the citizens of a nation is a policy that can never succeed. And, hopefully, South Africa will one day learn from the United States that diversity can be an element of strength in a free and vital nation.

GEORGE AND LOUISE SPINDLER
General Editors

Phlox, Wisconsin

Preface

This study is not about race relations, nor is it about civil rights. Particularly, it is not an attempt by a white man to explain the ways of black people. Rather, this is a study of how the universal need for group identity manifests itself in two geographically distant communities.

Recently, several observers have noted that black Americans who call for "black power" and make separatist demands are expressing a desire for cultural nationalism that is not unique to their minority situation. The national minorities of the Soviet Union (Moslem, Jew, Armenian, Latvian, and Tartar, to name only a few) struggle to keep their languages, cultures, and religions from being submerged by the dominant Great Russians. In Canada, French Canadians support efforts to win equality and even independence for their minority group. In Northern Ireland, Scotland, and Wales there is a continuing chorus of nationalism. In Belgium (Flemings and Walloons), Czechoslovakia (Slovaks and Czechs), Kenya (Luo and Kikuyu), and Nigeria (Ibo, Yoruba, and Hausa) there is an almost constant tension of intergroup animosity born of minority nationalism. Lately, such ethnic movements have begun to arise in the United States among Mexican-Americans, Indians, Asian-Americans, and, quite recently, among working-class people of Polish, Italian, and Slovakian descent.

Cultural nationalist movements have arisen in seeming contradiction to those who characterize the world as becoming a "global village." A reason for this rise in ethnocentric movements is that people generally find life more satisfactory if they are a part of a well-defined, significant group. Individuals clearly derive an added sense of identity from belonging to a community with shared customs and traditions. Apparently, the value one places on oneself is both directly and indirectly affected by the cohesiveness of, and pride in, one's group. If it is close-knit, the group lends a direct kind of support to the individual. If he comes from a proud group with a rich heritage, he will indirectly derive some sense of self-worth from its traditional strengths.

But the price of nationalism is often high. It opens the group to charges of clannishness. At the extreme, the price for nationalism may be the disintegration of the larger entity to which the group belongs. Ethnic separatism, whether it stems from a desire for the preservation of unique traits (as with the Jews in America) or a desire for a separate state (the Ibos in Nigeria), is functional for the group while at the same time presenting it with the risk of reaction from other groups who view the movement as a threat to national unity and integration.

Many black Americans, it appears, have decided to take this risk. Convinced that their social, political, and economic problems can only be solved through a nationalist movement, they are willing to pay the price of increased conflict with whites to achieve their ends. Similarly, the Cape Coloured people of

South Africa must now choose if they wish to continue pursuit of their historical desire to become a part of the white group in South Africa or to begin functioning as a separate group. The descriptions of black Los Angeles and Coloured Cape Town that I present in this case study are designed, therefore, to highlight the similarities and differences between two minority groups and to show how each is confronting the difficult questions of group identity.

The name Watts is used in this book to refer to the entire black community of Los Angeles. Although most of what is described did, indeed, occur in Watts proper, this neighborhood is not a self-contained community that, for the purposes of analysis, can always be usefully isolated from the rest of black Los Angeles. Similarly, Woodstock is often used as a shorthand reference for all the Coloured areas of Cape Town. As Watts is no more "typical" of black Los Angeles than any other nearby area, Woodstock is neither more nor less representative than any other Coloured area I might have chosen for the sake of convenience. Therefore, I occasionally blur distinctions between what happened in Watts proper and what happened in other black areas that surround it, as I also do between Woodstock proper and other Coloured areas of Cape Town. But to have dwelt on these differences (which, in any case, are marginal for our purposes) would have distracted from the central theme of the book, which transcends not only community but racial and national boundaries as well. These descriptions of "Watts" and "Woodstock" should be used by the reader, then, as illustrations of the general point that a positive sense of identity is necessary for a rewarding life, and not as community studies that seek to define the social lives of specific areas.

Most of the information about Watts was derived from my experience as a director of a tutorial project involving several hundred black children from South Central Los Angeles. In this program, founded in 1963, university students were recruited to tutor elementary and secondary school youths in reading and writing in a modest attempt to stem the tidal wave of school dropouts in the Los Angeles ghetto. In order to provide a more effective service for the children, I spent many hours questioning both their tutors and them about school and social problems of ghetto residents. Many discussions with black parents, teachers, and community leaders over a four-year period also contributed greatly to my understanding of the social structure and problems of the community.

Later, as a graduate student at Oxford University, I had several opportunities to meet and talk with South Africans about the racial situation in their country. These discussions whetted my curiosity to explore the parallels between race problems in the United States and South Africa. But I felt that I needed to make a more systematic study of Watts before I visited South Africa. I therefore returned to Los Angeles and spent four months interviewing leaders of the new groups that had arisen after the Watts riots. I then obtained a year's leave of absence from Oxford, and my wife and I travelled to South Africa on tourist visas. We rented a house in Cape Town and made our first contacts in the Coloured community using introductions we had acquired in England.

While in South Africa we attempted to obey all the laws of the country and at no time during our stay did we encounter any official or personal hostility from persons of any race. I easily found my way to the leaders of the Coloured community because of their desire for the world to know of their plight. I was always accompanied in my initial meetings with Coloureds by a trusted member of the community known not to be a government agent. Being a foreigner in South Africa was a bias in my favor and people quickly confided in me when word spread that I had "come from Oxford" to find out about their problems. I interviewed over a dozen leaders of the Cape Town Coloured community and talked at length to about fifty more people in their homes, in churches, or in my home. I also administered a questionnaire (with the aid of an Afrikaans-speaking Coloured woman) to gain quantitative evidence about the lives of poor Coloured families.

Acknowledgments

I cannot hope to acknowledge the help of all the people who made it possible for me to conduct and write this case study. But the most important individual was my wife, Marilyn, who participated in all aspects of research and preparation in the United States, South Africa, and England.

I would like to thank Dr. C. T. M. Hadwen of Guelph University, Ontario, for having introduced me to the problems of the black people of Los Angeles. His teachings are echoed throughout the book. Appreciation is similarly due to Mary Henry and Charles Daniel, community leaders who willingly and patiently educated me in the ways of black Los Angeles. Their friendship and advice were of incalculable value to my research.

I am grateful, particularly, to my Oxford thesis supervisors, Professor Kenneth Kirkwood and Dr. John Beattie, for their wise counsel, careful criticism, and always timely encouragement. I also wish to acknowledge the contributions of my doctoral examiners, Professor Maurice Freedman and Dr. Godfrey Lienhardt, for their helpful remarks on the thesis.

Gratitude is due to Professor Monica Wilson, Stanley Kahn, Gerald Stone, and Dr. Michael Whisson of the University of Cape Town for their hospitality and guidance during my stay in South Africa. Many of my ideas concerning the Coloured people are based on Dr. Whisson's research (but any shortcomings in the analysis are, of course, my responsibility).

Three talented writers, Dr. Elliott Liebow, Dr. Joel Rosenblatt, and Charles Lichenstein, read the manuscript carefully and offered cogent and sensitive suggestions for changes.

To Warden E. T. Williams and the Rhodes Trustees, my thanks for permission and funds to travel to South Africa. I would like also to thank Shirley Dixon for typing the final manuscript, and Christine Burrill who took the photographs of Watts.

Particularly, I would like to record the contribution my late mother, Irene O'Toole, made by typing the thesis and, together with my father James O'Toole, by helping me financially during the period of research.

Recognition and appreciation must be extended to the people of Watts and Woodstock who are, of course, the real authors of this book. I have tried to retell their stories faithfully as they told them to me and, in the retelling, have tried carefully to guard their privacy.

August 1972   JAMES O'TOOLE

Contents

WATTS AND WOODSTOCK

Introduction

On a demographer's map of Los Angeles there is a large black spot near the center of the city. Almost regardless of the criteria the demographer uses—crime rate, number of broken families, employment level, family income, education level, infant morality rate, incidence of venereal disease, or the color of the people—the area will be painted black. The nonwhite population (black and Mexican-American) comes close to having a corner on Los Angeles' social problems. In August 1965, the Negro area of the city was burnt as black as cartographer's ink. A riot on a sweltering summer day started in a neighborhood near the heart of the enormous black ghetto. That place, Watts, gave its name to the riot and, by association, to the entire black community of Los Angeles.

This community of 259,980[1] black Americans (of whom only 26,990 reside in Watts proper) does not match our conceptions of a slum or a ghetto. We picture the rows of drab, gardenless, identical houses and tenements of Glasgow, Birmingham, Paris, or New York when we think of a slum. We call to mind the walled Jewish district of Warsaw when we visualize a ghetto.

To the casual observer, South-Central Los Angeles is as far away in style from Warsaw or Glasgow as it is in miles. The streets here are palm-lined. The houses are separated by strips of grass. Each has a front and back lawn. It seems that every house has a car parked in front. Most houses have television antennas pointing toward the white world of nearby Hollywood, which beams out nightly entertainment. This is a unique slum, a strange ghetto.

The Cape Coloured people of South Africa, a "racial" amalgam of Bushmen, Hottentots, Negroes, Malaysians, Indians, and Europeans, inhabit an equally peculiar environment at the tip of the continent of Africa. In Cape Town they dwell amid poverty, disease, and crime in a slum of singular character near the center of the busy white Parliamentary capital of the Republic. There are 266,979[2] Coloureds living in the city (nearly a hundred thousand of them in central Cape Town—in District Six and Woodstock). Here, narrow streets wind up the foot of Table Mountain leading tortuously back on themselves past one- and two-story houses and shops with painted tin roofs, false fronts, gables and balconies,

---

[1] All Watts figures quoted in the study are from the U.S. Bureau of the Census, 1966.
[2] All Woodstock figures are based on South African Bureau of Statistics Yearbook, 1966.

1

scrolls and intricate lattice work, domes, gargoyles, and Doric, Corinthian, and Ionic capitals in haphazard combinations—all giving on some sordid square or unkempt garden. The Oriental blends and clashes with the Victorian, a peeling and crumbling return to the colonial past. Former respectability has now faded to squalor with all the charm of a doomed anachronism. Living in a different order of slum than the *favelas* of Rio de Janeiro, the ubiquitous *barrios* of other Latin American cities, or the shanty towns of new urban Africa, the Cape Coloured people have their own brand of impoverishment.

Although racially and linguistically different, the peoples of Watts and Woodstock were chosen for comparison because of the similarities between white South African and American cultures; because of the similarities between Cape Coloured society and black American society; and because of the similarities in social stratification in the two countries.

Both white groups have similar ideological histories emanating from an Anglo-Saxon colonial past coupled with Puritanism, the frontier intellect, individualism, and capitalism framed in the liberal terminology of the Enlightenment. The whites in both republics are composed, although in different proportions, of disparate ethnic groups (British, Irish, Dutch, French, German, Italian, Jewish), resulting in vigorous, "melting pot" immigrant states. South Africa and the United States are wealthy, industrial nations. In each, large numbers of people hold the view that nonwhites are morally and intellectually inferior to whites.

Cape Coloureds and black Americans have a common inheritance of slavery (manumission for Negroes occurred in 1863, for Coloureds in 1833). Most tribal customs and much of the culture of the Coloureds were destroyed in one generation, as was the case with American slaves. The second-generation Coloured slave was an Afrikaans-speaking Christian or Moslem; the second-generation American slave was an English-speaking Christian. Both groups have mixed racial backgrounds and represent about 10 percent of the total population of each country. Although they share Western culture with the dominant groups, they are separated from them by a color bar. The vast majority of both groups lives in a state of poverty relative to whites.

Historically, neither Cape Coloureds nor American Negroes have had a highly developed group-consciousness. Members of both groups tended to identify with the white population in their societies, and, consequently, denigrated their own groups in the process. Social scientists often use reference-group theory to show how men relate themselves to groups. Most commonly men relate to the groups of which they are members, but occasionally they may orient themselves toward groups other than their own. The social structure helps to determine the choice of reference group. In all stratified societies it is common to find those on the bottom choosing more prestigious strata as reference groups in the hope and belief that some of the status of the higher group will accrue to them. Black Americans and Coloureds commonly conformed to the values of those in the most prestigious ranks of their societies. Thus, blacks and Coloureds attempted as individuals to improve their self-images by trying to affiliate themselves with those at the top.

This process is called anticipatory socialization. In open societies it serves to help the individual rise into a higher group. At the same time, since the person has already accepted the values of the higher-ranking group, the process eases his adjustment to his new status. But anticipatory socialization frustrates individuals in racially closed social structures such as South Africa and, formerly, the United States. Anticipatory socialization is not fully functional in such social orders because the nonwhite individual would not be accepted by the group to which he aspires to belong and, also, because he would lose respect for, and acceptance by, his own group as a result of his orientation to white society.

This was the case with Watts blacks and Woodstock Coloureds who, to the degree they identified with whites, alienated themselves from their own groups. So many nonwhites became dissociated from their groups that the very ties of their communities disintegrated. The "false consciousness" of blacks and Coloureds who identified with white groups led to a kind of nonwhite group alienation. In trying to affiliate with a higher-status group, the individual must depreciate his own group, and eventually depreciate himself when he finds he cannot enter the group with which he identifies. Both the group and the individual suffer a loss of self-esteem, and experience a sense of alienation and anomie.

The sociologist Émile Durkheim identified anomie as the condition of relative normlessness in a group. It is, indeed, the lack of a state of community that occurs when the social structure prevents people from realizing the norms of the culture. For example, the people in Watts historically could not achieve the culturally prescribed goal of success in the United States—they could not, in effect, realize the American Dream. Yet the American Dream is the first important cultural lesson most American children are taught. The African child typically learns what his obligations are to his age mates and kin and the name of his totem and what it stands for; the upper-class British child learns the histories of his kings and the characters in Shakespeare; the American child learns that he can and must climb to the top of his society. Most Americans are taught and believe that through hard work and perseverance they will "make it to the top." The Watts child, who saw on television the white man's automated home with its swimming pool in the back yard, learned his lesson at almost the age the white child learned his. "I'm gonna get me some of the good life," they said in Watts. But only rarely did poor blacks in Watts get a taste of the good life. And because they learned that they could and should achieve material success, they took their failures to do so personally. Both Watts and Woodstock, then, were afflicted with a kind of rootlessness that stems from the inability of the individual either to enter fully into the life of the group with which he identifies or to realize the aspirations he has been told were his to achieve.

Much of this book is history. In the first two sections situations are described in Watts that in many ways no longer exist. The day when blacks cowered before whites now seems far in the past. Inherent in this historical yet recent change is a lesson of enduring importance: Central to a satisfying life is the possession of high self-esteem. It is clear from the experience of black Americans that an individual must be able to respect himself before he can cope with the problems that beset his life.

Our personal identity depends upon our mirror image. If others see us as inferior, we see ourselves as inferior. Most important, it is equally true that if we view ourselves with pride, others will tend to respect us. There is no arcane process involved in this mirror game. The lesson of identity is clear and simple: Thinking makes it so. Blacks remained in "niggerdom" because whites viewed them as inferiors —and blacks accepted this stereotype of the majority group. When blacks began to have self-respect, to believe that they could have power and beauty, they began to acquire these things. White attitudes changed at the same time—for example, the word "nigger" was less apt to be heard among whites after the black man became self-assertive.

To change the identity of a group often requires the reformulation of myth. When black power myths were substituted for white racialist myths, the image of blacks changed in their own eyes and in the eyes of others. Clearly, myth plays an important part in personality formation. People tend to become what they are taught to believe they are. But an individual, because of racial, economic, and other social factors, cannot be trained to be different from what society expects him to be. Identity, then, also rests greatly on the image of the group to which the individual belongs. Individuals learn their social roles both from their parents and from the larger groups of which they are members. It was not enough, therefore, for a black mother to teach her son that he was equal to whites, because the black group to which he belonged was perceived to be inferior. To change the role of the black individual in society, the perception of the black group in general had to change first. The concept of identifying with the entire black community had to replace the past practice of the individual identifying with white society. To achieve a healthy identity for all black individuals, the concept of the group had to be strengthened.

Almost all groups think of themselves in terms of "we." All groups have names for themselves that exclude others. In this respect, Cape Coloured people are unique. They seldom refer to themselves as a group. If forced to name themselves, some say "the so-called Coloureds." American Negroes today are debating if they should call themselves blacks, Negroes, Africans, or Afro-Americans. The search for identity, then, can be as basic as the name of a people itself.

Ruth Benedict (1934) has said, "What really binds men together is their culture —the ideas and the standards they have in common." It would seem that both black Americans and Cape Coloureds are people struggling to find the things they can be proud of that will bind them together as groups. Self-image is related to group image in both Watts and Woodstock. When all the individuals in a group view themselves in a certain manner, this viewpoint is also the collective view of the group. This is the group's concept of itself—its identity. The way a group sees itself contributes to the attitudes it holds toward its power, purposes, duties, and responsibilities—indeed, toward its entire role both as a binding force among its members and as the united front it presents to the outside world. The entire functioning of the group is intricately tied to its self-image. The Masai of East Africa, for example, see themselves as a distinct and superior tribe of brave hunters. This pride was at least in part responsible for their being able to ignore the outstretched paternalistic hand of the European colonizer and his offer of civilization. Even today, the Masai, more than any other tribe, flout the *harambee* ("let us pull together") spirit in independent Kenya and Tanzania. Conversely, blacks and

Coloureds who accept a culture that calls them "boy" become dependent on whites for their leadership and livelihood. The internal functioning of their groups is affected by the image they have of themselves and their groups.

This study of Watts and Woodstock is from the particular viewpoint of a social anthropologist. The reader will find that the disoriented cultures of Watts and Woodstock are not examined in an historical or psychological framework. The social functioning of these communities is explained in terms of their social structures and the greater social structures that encompass them. Underlying the descriptions of the societies presented here is the assumption that the various parts of a social system are complexly interrelated. For example, the social roles that black people play in America are related to other factors in the society—for example, to the economic, family, and political systems. It is not a coincidence that unemployed black men tend to have low self-esteem, exhibit little political awareness, and experience great difficulty in maintaining stable households. This interrelationship of social factors also has important implications for change. For if one significant factor is changed, this change will have repercussions in other parts of the system. For example, in this case study, we see how the use of the black power myth has been used as a social lever in Watts to change unsatisfactory political and familial institutions.

In Part One I examine the family patterns found in preriot Watts and in Woodstock. Among the overwhelming majority of poor people in both areas, the relative absence of a strong marital bond has led to the prominence of a matrifocal family pattern. Most important, in both communities the weakness of the conjugal tie is compensated by strong kinship ties, particularly the mother-child bond. The people of both Watts and Woodstock argue that the systems in which they live prevent them from having the kind of family organization they would choose for themselves. Although they are particularly proud of the remarkable way their women have compensated for the frequent absences of men from their households, they would prefer to live in a system that provides greater incentives for families to stay together.

The main systemic block to family stability is that both Coloured and black men have great difficulty finding the kind of steady employment needed to support a family. Thus, in both Watts and Woodstock we find a relation between unemployment or low-income of fathers and broken homes. For example, in Watts, where underemployment of working-age men in 1965 ran as high as 40 percent, it was not surprising to find the father absent in 39 percent of the families. (There was not, of course, a perfect correlation between underemployment and absent fathers, but it appeared to have been quite high.) The nature of the employment available to black men is also a factor that affects family stability. In 27 percent of the families *with* male heads, earnings at the time of the riot were nevertheless below the government poverty line. Since the median family income in the community ($3,771) was barely above the poverty line, it was often found that the father was unable to protect the members of his family from hunger, the elements, and even physical harm. Either he was too poor to fulfill these functions or he was absent when he was needed. The onus fell, therefore, on the mother, who then became the "instrumental leader" (see Glossary) of the family, with subsequent further

loss of self-esteem for the father. This is not to imply a necessary correlation between unemployment and family disorganization in Watts and Woodstock. There
were stable families headed by unemployed men in both communities, but this was
not the usual case. And, contrary to popular belief, the matrifocal family structure
was not wholly confined to the lower classes. Although superficially similar to the
middle-class white norm, many middle-class black and Coloured families were
mother-dominated because of the nonwhite man's lower economic and social status.

In Part Two I suggest that the political institutions of preriot Watts and Woodstock were led by whites or by nonwhite women. In the cases where nonwhite men
had influence, these men were found to be ministers who derived their power from
the support of whites or from nonwhite women. Again, this problem was a consequence of the role nonwhite men played in the economic and political systems of
their nations. In both cases, the nonwhite man played only a marginal, subordinate
role even in his own subgroup. His low status and resultant low self-esteem made
it difficult for him to take part in effective nonwhite political organizations. The
male political role was often abdicated to women or co-opted by whites.

Blacks and Coloureds historically lacked the confidence to organize to overcome
their powerlessness. The result of believing that they were unable to govern themselves had disastrous consequences for their groups as wholes. For example, neither
in preriot Watts nor in Woodstock could one find the minimal degree of political
activity required for the smooth functioning of the group or for major social
change. Neither were independent, self-sufficient communities in the classical
sense. White institutions, values, and culture permeated the nonwhite communities
and influenced their functioning in untoward ways. Watts and Woodstock were
communities containing "foreign" organizations—the police, schools, welfare
agencies, and some churches—which were a part of the white world, administered
by whites, and placed in the community with or without the consent of the people.
Therefore, institutions that seemed uniquely "black" or "Coloured" may have
arisen in response to white pressures.

The most significant consequence of this external penetration into Watts and
Woodstock was that neither community was able to organize internally in order
to foster group cohesion. The communities became dysfunctional because they had
few indigenous secondary institutions to bind them together. The result in both
Watts and Woodstock was a kind of dis-ease, a social malaise manifested in self-
hatred, crime, drink, and other forms of deviant and retreatist behavior.

In Part Three I demonstrate how the people of Watts are attempting to overcome
problems of personal, family, and social disorganization. They hope to overcome these problems by creating a cultural nationalism that will lead to racial
and self-pride. The impetus for this nationalism came about, in part, because
of a gradual liberalization in the white community, which for the first time permitted blacks to act in other than traditional subservient roles. These new roles, of
which the black power leader is the most obvious manifestation, often embrace
traditional white middle-class behavior. For example, Watts blacks are now dem-
onstrating political initiative and demanding the same rights of self-government
historically enjoyed by whites. The leaders of Watts are attempting to overcome
the self-hatred of blacks evidenced by drug addiction, crime, and cosmetic pro-

cesses performed in order to appear white. In short, blacks are beginning to act with the self-confidence that has heretofore been the prerogative of whites. To achieve these ends some blacks have found it expedient to preach the superiority of black over white. But even this may be interpreted as a modification of traditional white behavior.

In the concluding chapter, the black nationalism of Watts is contrasted to the white bias of the people of Woodstock. Even though the social status of the Coloured people is deteriorating, they still retain a dysfunctional attachment to whites as their reference group. But the political realities of *apartheid* are beginning to force change on the people of Woodstock.

Time and what it measures, change, are essential aspects of this study. Because the rate of change in Watts has been so rapid since the 1965 riot, time must be considered as a limitation to the study. The analysis of Watts must be considered "historical" in that it deals with a research period extending from September 1963 to September 1969. The speed of change is so great in Watts, in fact, that this or any other such study must be outdated before it is read. To partially compensate for this limiting factor, the chapters on Watts in Parts One and Two deal with the community immediately *before the riot* in August 1965, stopping the clock at that eventful moment in the community's history. Part Three is an account of recent social change in Watts. The chapters on Woodstock cover the period from the winter of 1967 to May 1968, the month in which the Coloured people of South Africa lost their representation in Parliament.

PART ONE | Self-Image and Family Roles

1 / The Cape Coloured people

I realized that the Bible had been written by white men. I knew that, according to many Christians, I was a descendant of Ham, who had been cursed, and that I was therefore predestined to be a slave. This had nothing to do with anything I was, or contained, or could become; my fate had been sealed forever, from the beginning of time.[1]

The history of the Cape Coloured people traces the transformation of several diverse racial stocks of free people into one enslaved, despised group—the children of Ham. *"Ons is Gam"* (We are Ham), the Coloured people say in self-deprecation. The whites call them *"Hotnots"* (from Hottentot).

The well-documented history of these hapless people is neither pleasant nor dramatic (See especially Marais, 1957). Before the Dutch came to the Cape, the warm, sparse lands there were inhabited by bands of Hottentots and Bushmen with whom the first Dutch explorers in 1652 attempted to trade. Soon, however, true to the universal pattern of colonization, the Dutch slaughtered many of the indigenous people of the Cape and enslaved the rest or drove them off their lands. However, the Hottentots were regarded, according to Marais, as "unsuitable and inadequate" to meet the demand for labor in the Cape, so groups of slaves were introduced into the colony, first by the Dutch and later by the British. Blacks from Mozambique, East Africa, and Madagascar and Asians from Ceylon, Indonesia, and India were added to the slave population in the rapidly expanding Cape Colony. To this gene pool was added the "blood" of Europeans as a result of illicit unions with port sailors and Dutch farmers. From this exotic amalgam of races the Coloured people were born. To this day a branch of the Coloureds has continued to refer to itself as the Bastards. This unfortunate name is perhaps more descriptively accurate than Cape Coloured. Marais (1957) has noted that no less than 75 percent of the children born to Cape slave mothers in the first years of settlement were half-breeds.

From the beginning of the European settlement of the Cape the aboriginal peoples were often thought of as "things" and as "animals." Marais reports that Boer farmers have historically referred to Coloured children as *kleingoed,* small goods or things, which may be comparatively more humane than the English

[1] James Baldwin, *The Fire Next Time* (New York: Dell Publishing Company, Inc., 1962), p. 53.

11

magistrate who preferred to refer to Hottentots and Bushmen as "game" as late as 1879.

From the start, the Coloureds were used by the whites as "buffers" against the streams of Africans migrating into the Cape from the north. Coloured communities at the far reaches of the frontier spared the whites the full brunt of Zulu and Xhosa onslaughts. Coloureds were also used extensively as soldiers in white commando groups fighting Africans.

Through religious preaching and efficacious paternalism, the Coloureds quickly came to accept the superiority and leadership of the whites, not only when fighting against Africans but in direct Coloured-white relations. In 1890 the British governor in the Cape wrote that laws specifically applicable to the Coloureds must tend to "perpetuate [them] as an inferior and distinct people." Perhaps no colonial policy has ever borne fruit more successfully. Early in the history of the Cape an invidious distinction between "civilized" and "noncivilized" people was established. The civilized man, by virtue of his purportedly advanced culture, was to be accorded respect. But in South Africa "civilized" had, in fact, little to do with culture. "Civilized" was, and is still today, a South African synonym for "white." The Coloured people quickly learned that they, the children of Ham, could never become civilized because they could never become white. As "an inferior and distinct people" they have remained on the margin of "civilized" society, a "brown-appendage," as Marais (1957) has called them, of the European group in South Africa.

As early as 1851, it was said that the Coloureds had learned to despise their own people. According to Marais, they had learned to have a "childlike faith in the integrity of the white man," due largely to the paternalistic attitude of the British government. The British emancipated the Coloured people, but they left an unofficial color bar which proved to be just as effective in subjugating the Coloureds. Still, the official act of freeing the slaves left the Coloureds in debt to the British. The British then capitalized on the Coloureds' loyalty by enfranchising them and using their votes to offset a Boer majority in the Cape. But once peace had been made with the Boer, the British began the task of disfranchising the Coloured man.

A reading of the history of the early Cape leaves one with the vivid impression that the Coloured man was treated at all times as a means to various ends, as a tool, as nothing more than a thing. The early history of the Coloured people was, in effect, the systematic creation of an inferior race that would be dependent upon whites for its culture, livelihood, and leadership. The traditional cultures of the various groups who became known as the Coloureds seem to have vanished a generation after enslavement. During slavery, Coloured people readily became "Eurafricans"—European in language, religion, and culture, African in color and birthplace only.

Emancipation meant little to the Coloured man. He merely passed from slavery into serfdom. Serfdom in South Africa was, and to some extent is today, every bit as pernicious as slavery, in part because of a practice called, harmlessly enough, "the tot system." Behind this jolly phrase lies a system that guarantees the total debasement of a human being. Under the tot system, laborers are given alcohol as part of their wages. Starting in the early morning, Coloured field workers are given tots of wine at various intervals throughout the day. This practice keeps the worker in a stupor that leaves him tractable but not so drunk that he falls asleep. A Boer told Marais (1957) that he "employed no Coloured man who did not drink. The tot drinker would do for a tot what the nondrinker would not do for a shilling." In general, the tot system reinforces other systems in South African society because it keeps the Coloured man at menial rural work and content with his lot or, at least, dependent and ineffectual.

When one reads Marais' history of the Coloured people, one is struck by how few Coloureds are mentioned by name. Marais' history is the story of the white man's policies and attitudes toward the Coloureds. There are few Coloured actors in his book. The Coloured people have had little influence over their own history. There are no Coloured heroes in South Africa. There is only one statue in all of South Africa of a Coloured man, and he was neither an important figure nor, strictly speaking, a Cape Coloured.[2]

One is hard pressed to find instances of Coloureds in control of their own destiny. Only in their decision to migrate to the cities have they demonstrated any will of their own that runs contrary to the official policies of the whites. In 1904, half of the Coloured population lived in rural areas in the Cape. By 1960, less than one third remained in the *platteland*. To be sure, this shift was mainly in response to better-paying jobs in the cities and the mechanization of the farms, but the move was nevertheless remarkable because it went against the urgings of the government, which was finding it increasingly difficult to cope with the migration.

RACIAL CLASSIFICATION

Contemporary South African society is stratified into four primary racial categories: African, white, Coloured, and Asian. Each group is internally segmented: the Africans tribally, the whites between the English-speaking group and the Afrikaners, the Coloureds in half a dozen segments (discussed later), and the Asians mainly between Moslems and Hindus. The difference between the primary stratification and the internal stratification is that the former is legal while the latter is customary.

After Africans (68.1 percent) and whites (19.0 percent), the Coloureds are the third largest group in South Africa, comprising a little less than 10 percent of the population. In Cape Town Municipality, however, they are the largest ethnic group, (making up about 54 percent of the total population). Twenty-five percent of all Coloureds in the Republic live in greater Cape Town.

The legal division of the population of the Republic into four groups is arbitrary. The population could have been divided just as logically (or illogically) into two or twenty-two groups. The major difficulty inherent in the present system of classification and stratification in South Africa is that many individuals do not fit exactly into any one of the four primary racial groups. This problem is particularly perplexing to the Coloureds, many of whom have either white skin or black skin and can easily be taken for an Afrikaner in the first instance or an African in the

---

[2] The statue is of Adam Kok, a so-called Griqua (a racially mixed group with a genealogical history distinct from the Cape Coloureds).

second. To the Coloureds, these racial distinctions appear as life and death issues. This state of affairs seems so patently ridiculous to non-South Africans, who seldom are so concerned with slight variations in skin color, that it is hard for outsiders to sympathize with the Coloured man's dilemma.

It is indeed difficult for outsiders to understand the full consequences of an individual's racial classification in South Africa. But, for the South African, racial classification deeply affects his life chances. If a light-skinned Coloured man is reclassified as white, for example, his salary will double almost overnight, he will become eligible for increased public and social services, his children will receive a proper schooling with the possibility of a university education, he will be able to travel abroad, he will be enfranchised, he will be able to attend cinemas, churches, restaurants, and clubs that were previously closed to him. All this can happen through the whim of a government official who is empowered to decide his color. The white official may be of darker complexion than the Coloured man, but he has the right to declare the man an inferior or to accept him into the dominant group. Similarly, if a dark-skinned Coloured man were to be reclassified as an African (something that seldom happens), he would immediately lose his home, his job, his freedom of movement within South Africa, and his right to freehold land and would be forced to live under conditions he would find intolerable.

It would be helpful at this point to define the various racial groups in South Africa in order that the reader may more readily grasp what is admittedly a strange concept. However, definition is difficult because South Africans themselves have never been able to agree on the characteristics that distinguish one race from another. In 1950, the South African government made an attempt to define the various races for purposes of the Population Registration Act, which was to fix forever racial distinctions in the Republic. A white person was defined as "a person who in appearance obviously is, or who is generally accepted as, a White person, but does not include a person who, although in appearance obviously a White person, is generally accepted as a Coloured person."

A white man is therefore described as one who looks like a white man and is accepted as white by other whites. This description certainly is not very helpful because it begs the question by not describing what a white person is supposed to look and act like. The definition of a Coloured man is more confusing because it is entirely negative. We are not told what a Coloured man is, but rather what he is not. According to the definition given in the Pensions Act of 1928, the Coloureds are defined as a residue, a catch-all race:

A Coloured person means any person who is neither white nor
(a)   A Turk or a member of a race or tribe in Asia; nor
(b)   A member of an aboriginal race or tribe of Africa; nor
(c)   A Hottentot, Bushman or Koronna; nor
(d)   A person who is residing in a native location ... under the
        same conditions as a native; nor
(e)   An American Negro.

The reader will have to be satisfied with this imperfect definition, since there is no accepted definition that can tell us who the Coloured man is, rather than who he is not. If the reader can imagine his confusion magnified to the extent that it becomes the primary source of conflict in his life, he will then begin to understand what it means to be Coloured in South Africa. The members of this residual group—black, white, brown, and yellow; Moslem and Christian; sophisticated and unsophisticated; poor and rich—have only one thing in common to bind them together: they are all discriminated against in the same way. The blatant and complex discrimination in the political sphere is discussed in a later chapter. The present inquiry is concerned with those aspects of discriminaton in employment, housing, education, social services, and civil rights that determine the collective characteristics and shared fate of the group.

EMPLOYMENT

Employment is the crucial factor in the status placement of Coloured men. *Apartheid* laws in South Africa prevent Coloureds from holding many skilled and semiskilled positions. The first comprehensive policy of segregation in South Africa was the so-called Civilized Labor Policy of 1924. The intent of this policy was to insure that no nonwhite could be hired until all whites in the society were employed. Nonwhites were to be hired only as a last resort. The rule was a legalization of the customary "last hired, first fired" principle regarding nonwhites. The policy differentiated between peoples with European living standards and those with primitive requirements. But the policy was quickly applied to Coloureds, despite the fact that they were obviously "civilized" by the government's own standards.

The rule forced Coloureds into manual labor positions where they are at a disadvantage in competition with Africans, who will work for a lower wage. Recently, however, the government has taken the Civilized Labor Policy to its logical extreme by reserving some occupations for Coloureds at the expense of the Africans. In addition, there is now a nascent policy of removing Africans from the Cape Peninsula, which will, if implemented, eventually improve the position of the unskilled Coloured worker (with accompanying disastrous effects for the African worker).

The type of job generally available to a Coloured man today is piecework, with little or no security and low wages (approximately 2 rand, or $2.80 per day). Most white men in South Africa have professional, technical, administrative, or clerical positions. Many also own farms. Coloureds, however, are mainly farm and production workers or semiskilled and unskilled laborers. For example, in 1966 there were only sixty-nine Coloured doctors and dentists (compared with 6,797 white) in all of South Africa. At the lowest end of the occupational scale there were 86,146 "laborers" among Coloured men, but only 13,146 among whites (even though there are twice as many whites as Coloureds in South Africa). The only profession in which there is a sizable representation of Coloured men is teaching. In fact, "teacher" and "middle class" are almost synonymous among Coloureds in Cape Town. However, in some skilled and semiskilled jobs, such as footwear, clothing and furniture manufacturing, and bricklaying, Coloureds dominate entire industries in the western Cape. A sizable number of Coloureds is also employed in the printing trade, although their numbers are dwindling due to job reservations for whites and the increasing cooperation of unions with the government in keeping Coloureds out of certain occupational fields.

The incomes of Coloureds reflect their status in the employment hierarchy. Per capita income for whites is nearly nine times that of Coloureds. In the few industries where Coloureds and whites do the same jobs, whites earn about two times the salary of Coloureds. Employment is an important issue because it is the key to the power of Coloured women in some lower-class households. Because the men cannot earn enough to support their families, a great many Coloured women must work. Nearly half of those employed are domestic servants. Because Coloured men do not have access to well-paying jobs, they often become dependent upon women for a great part of their livelihood.

HOUSING

Prior to the Group Areas Act of 1950, there was no legislation restricting neighborhoods where Coloureds could live in Cape Town. This does not mean that Coloureds enjoyed complete residential integration. Middle- and upper-class white neighborhoods historically have been segregated (except for the shacks and quarters of servants). But the lower-class areas of Cape Town appear to have been integrated. The areas of Woodstock and adjoining Salt River still had large numbers of poor white inhabitants living next door to Coloureds in 1967–1968. This last vestige of residential integration will not last much longer, however. The policy of the Nationalist Government is to achieve total residential segregation. The government has been gradually declaring Coloured areas in Cape Town for whites only and has been moving Coloureds out of white areas. The process is slow and has not met with much cooperation from either Coloured or white Capetonians. The important fact is that today Coloureds can legally reside only in areas specifically set aside for them. Almost all of these areas are government-built and operated townships in undesirable locations some distance from the center of Cape Town.

The homes of Coloureds range from two-room wood buildings with tin roofs to comfortable middle-class dwellings similar to the homes of many whites in Cape Town. Most of the homes, however, fall between these extremes. A typical home for a family of six would have two bedrooms-cum-living rooms and a kitchen and a bathroom with a small rear garden and a tiny front garden. Most of the houses of this type were built of brick and plaster at the turn of the century. They have tin roofs and little ventilation, making them very hot in summer and cold in winter.

Some Coloureds still live in *pondokkies,* tin and wooden one-room shacks without electricity, running water, or sanitary facilities. By the government's own standards, as many as 50 percent of the Coloured people may live in substandard housing.

Some Coloured people live in pondokkies *on the Cape sand flats.*

EDUCATION

Historically, Coloured education was the preserve of missionary and church schools. In this century, however, the government has gradually taken over the task of educating Coloured children. Today, virtually all Coloured children in Cape Town are in government schools. Until 1963, Coloured education was administered by the same local authorities who were responsible for white schools. Now, Coloured education falls under the aegis of the Department of Coloured Affairs, a government agency charged with preserving the separate identity of the Coloured group. The Department has greatly limited the freedom of teachers in Coloured schools to teach not only what they want but the language in which they teach it. The Department's unwritten policy is to conduct all classes in Afrikaans rather than in English—the preferred language of nearly all Coloured students. One purpose of teaching in Afrikaans, it seems, is to reduce the number of Coloureds who can qualify for education abroad where they might, and often do, pick up "radical" ideas. This policy also tends to limit the reading material of the Coloureds

—newspapers, books, and magazines—to those written in Afrikaans. These publications are almost exclusively pro-*apartheid*. Thus, the teaching of Afrikaans to Coloureds is a successful method of social control.

There is no compulsory education for Coloureds, yet most Coloured children in Cape Town probably attend school until they are about fourteen. There is a separate syllabus for each racial group in South Africa. A special curriculum for Coloured primary schools in the Cape had been in existence since 1923, but the primary difference between it and the white curriculum was that the Coloured course was simpler and more practically-oriented than the white syllabus. The effect was to minimize the number of Coloured university applicants. Under legislation passed by the Nationalist Government, however, Coloured schools now have become agents of *apartheid*. Teaching the innate right of white leadership has become an essential part of the curriculum. According to *The Primary School Course Syllabus in Environment Study* used in the Cape,

> The aim of school activity is to give the child a clear idea of himself in the socio-economic structure of his country and, more specifically, the place taken in it by the particular section to which his family group belongs and in addition the economic and cultural values of his particular section. . . .

As in other societies, the aim of schooling in South Africa is to perpetuate the social system of the nation—in this case the system of racial hierarchy. This aim is achieved by giving the inferior peoples inferior education. In 1950, the annual government expenditure for education per white pupil in South Africa was nearly three times that for Coloureds. These figures, however, do not tell the whole story, because a far greater percentage of whites is enrolled in schools than are Coloureds, and most Coloureds drop out before reaching secondary school. Only a fortunate few attend universities.

SOCIAL SERVICES

The social status of Coloureds is determined in part by inferior social services that cement their rank in the racial hierarchy. Although Coloureds pay taxes at the same rate as whites, they do not receive the same social services in return. For example, the rate at which welfare grants are dispensed is differentiated racially. All pensions, disability grants, and child maintenance grants in South Africa pay about twice as much for white individuals.

The Coloured people are particularly handicapped in the area of health services. There is no national health service in South Africa and, even though Groote Schuur Hospital (made famous by Dr. Christiaan Barnard's heart transplant operations) adjoins Woodstock, there was no extensive system of free clinics for Coloureds in Cape Town during the period of research. The consequences of this neglect are profoundly demonstrated in figures for life expectancy (twenty years less for Coloureds than whites) and infant mortality (four times higher among Coloureds). In addition, for Coloureds the death rate associated with diseases such as tuberculosis and syphilis, which are linked with poverty and can be cured through medical care, is six to twelve times that of whites.

CIVIL RIGHTS

Many laws can be described that limit the civil rights of Coloureds. It is necessary here to touch on only a few of the myriad pieces of *apartheid* policies and legislation in South Africa. There is segregation in public places such as sport fields, beaches, parks, and public buildings. Public transportation—trains, buses, and taxis—is segregated. There is *apartheid* in private establishments—shops, hotels, restaurants, and cinemas. Finally, there is *apartheid* of the dead, since cemeteries are racially segregated. Following is a list of the major statutes that over the years have been drawing ever finer the line between Coloureds and whites:

1922 Apprenticeship Act—Restricted Coloureds' opportunity to enter some trades
1924 Civilized Labor Policy—Insured that whites would be hired before nonwhites
1925 Wage Act—Removed competitive advantage of Coloureds willing to work for a smaller salary than whites
1949 Mixed Marriages Act—Barred Coloureds from marrying whites
1950 Immorality Act—Made sexual intercourse illegal between whites and nonwhites
1950 Population Registration Act—Provided that every South African be classified according to his race and that he carry a card identifying his race
1950 Group Areas Act—Segregated residential areas
1956 South African Act—Provided for a separate voters' roll for Coloureds
1963 Coloured Persons Education Act—Put Coloured education under the Department of Coloured Affairs
1968 Representation of Coloured Persons—Segregated the Coloured group politically by removing its representatives from Parliament.

The purpose of these laws is to ossify the racial hierarchy by securing the perpetual inferiority of the Coloured people. As we have seen, *apartheid* laws concerning education and employment successfully serve this end. But petty *apartheid,* such as segregation in public places, is also a useful tool because it effectively destroys the dignity of the Coloured man. Three examples illustrate this clearly: (1) A prime complaint about *apartheid* among Coloureds is the mundane problem of finding a toilet. All toilets are marked either *slegs blankes,* whites only, or *nie-blankes,* nonwhites. The humiliating circumstance in which Coloured people often find themselves is that in most places no *nie-blankes* facilities are provided. (2) In Cape Town there is a bus that is integrated as it runs through Woodstock and District Six, but when it enters the white downtown area it stops and the driver waits for all the Coloureds on the bottom floor of the omnibus to move to the top before he continues. Another bus, affectionately dubbed "the Chameleon" by Coloureds, has folding signs over each seat saying *slegs blankes.* As the bus fills up and as need dictates, the conductor puts the flaps down, giving whites first priority of the available seats. (3) This incident was described by a Coloured man: "I took my little daughters for a walk along the promenade by the ocean. It was a hot day and when the girls spotted a cafe that served ice cream, they implored, 'Daddy, buy us an ice cream.' I was faced with a terrible dilemma. Must I feign sternness and deny them the ice cream outright, or tell them that they are Coloured and are not welcome in that establishment?"

In summary, it can be said that in order to maintain a strict correlation between status and color, the whites of South Africa have imposed *apartheid* laws. The end result of *apartheid* is to reduce the Coloureds to permanent inferiors by proving to them that they are "uncivilized." This is accomplished through laws designed to limit their opportunities for advancement. Poor schooling, inferior social services, and, most important, an effective check on economic advancement through segregation in employment insure the continuing dominance of whites in South Africa.

STRATIFICATION WITHIN THE COLOURED GROUP

Government Proclamation 46 of 1959 (amended in 1961) states that the Coloured group in South Africa includes "Cape Coloureds," "Cape Malays," "Griquas," "Chinese," "Indians" (but only those who are not classified as Asians), "Other Asiatics," and "Other Coloureds." Just exactly what an "other Asiatic" or an "other Coloured" is we are not told. One searches in vain for anyone in either category in Woodstock. In Cape Town, the Coloureds themselves readily acknowledge only two specific categories, Christians and Moslems (whom whites often group together under the name "Malays"). The Moslems compose about 6 percent of the Coloured population. The true "Malay" among them are descendants of political exiles from the Dutch East Indies, and are often skilled artisans. Many Cape Coloureds, however, are of the Islamic religion but are not members of the Malay group. They may be full members of the Coloured group, as are many among the small Indian community in Cape Town. In other words, stratification is not as neatly defined as the government proclamation would have it. Sometimes an Indian is a Coloured and sometimes he is not. To the people of Woodstock, other factors besides the official group a man belongs to are far more important in determining his social status.

Since status advancement for Coloureds in the general system of stratification is blocked, an intense separate hierarchical system within the group has developed. Because race is the most important social factor in South African society, it is natural that racial traits should predominate in the internal stratification of the Coloured group. Among Coloureds there is a hierarchy based on the general rule that the whiter you are, the higher you are. This rule is mitigated somewhat by such determinants of class differentiation as economic standing, occupation, language group, religion, and education. An analysis follows of the major criteria used by Coloureds in evaluating other Coloureds and themselves.

PHYSICAL TRAITS

A favorite pastime among Coloured people of all classes is the recitation of their genealogies. But the form the recitation takes is of little use to the anthropologist interested in familial roles, because Coloured people bias their genealogies in favor of their white ancestors. When the discussion of relatives is introduced into a conversation, a Coloured will often say, "My grandfather was white" and launch into an extended biography of the man. It often turns out that the man was not white but rather had white "blood." Any "blood" to which Coloureds might refer is invariably white. Hottentot, African, or Asian ancestors are incidental to any discussion of descent. There is no status value, for example, in having an African grandmother. One comes away from such a genealogical discussion with the general impression that many Coloured people are descended by a neat biological trick from only one (white) ancestor.

Coloureds are acutely aware of slight differences in skin shade. This may coincide with the propensity of the government to reclassify people according to color. If a man looks white, there is a temptation for him to try to "pass" into the white group. Passing is another extremely popular topic of conversation among Coloureds, almost all of whom claim to have relatives living as whites. A prime complaint among Coloureds is that the Race Classification Act divides families because nervous "white" relatives cannot risk being seen visiting Coloured relatives. But most Coloureds are ambivalent about passing. They say that passing is beneficial for one's children because it enables them to attend better schools. On the other hand, it is detrimental to community spirit because it causes the passer to "feel superior to his old friends."

The extent of passing is difficult to estimate with any accuracy. Due to the strict laws of *apartheid*, there probably is far less passing now than before the Race Classification Act came into force. Although the claims of the Coloureds are probably inflated for obvious ego-boosting reasons, even a casual observer can tell that many white South Africans are, in fact, Coloured. Because of this inconsistency in racial differentiation in South Africa, terms like "white" and "Coloured" lose their traditional meaning. Among the people of Woodstock there exists a complex calculus of status ranking, in which skin shade and physical features are correlated with Caucasian features and skin color on the positive axis and Hottentot and Negro features and color on the negative. The meaning of the category "white" varies with the context in which it is used. When a Coloured refers to his "white" brother, he may mean his legally classified white brother or his lighter-skinned brother or even his brother with white features and dark skin. A Coloured will often say about someone of the same color that he is "darker" than himself. This is what Freud calls "the narcissism of small differences." To the Coloured man, acutely aware of the value of "whiteness," there exists a real difference that to the non-South African appears as merely a perceived difference. It is said that Eskimos see different "colors" of snow. The phenomena may not be entirely unrelated. Race classification is as important to the life chances (if not the survival) of the

Coloured man as knowledge of the snow is important to the Eskimo. Both snow in the Arctic and race in South Africa are overwhelming factors that individuals must cope with in order to succeed in the environment.

In summary, color is by far the most important factor in the determination of class among Coloureds. White skin is viewed as a panacea for all of an individual's personal problems, as an open-sesame to monetary success, love, and self-esteem. And it appears to be true, but not on a one-to-one correlation, that the wealthiest, most successful Coloureds do tend to have light skin. The Coloureds explain this by saying that light-skinned Coloureds are given better chances by color-conscious whites (and, perhaps, by color-conscious Coloureds). This may or may not be true, but it is certain that light complexion often coincides with other positive traits, such as educational achievement, use of the English language, and membership in the Anglican Church.

OCCUPATION AS A CLASS DETERMINANT

Only the few thousand teachers, ministers, professional people, and skilled workers among the Coloureds constitute a middle class by South African European standards. This group comprises only about 3 percent of the Colored population. One reason economic security is prized among Coloureds is that it affords the opportunity of living like whites. It is not altogether inaccurate to view Coloured society as a continuum, with the wealthier people on one end of the scale living under physical conditions that resemble those of the white middle class and expressing allegiance to the values and attitudes of whites and the poor people at the other end of the scale living under primitive conditions with, at least partly, their own values and norms. Although this is not an entirely verifiable description of the society, it is one held by most Coloureds, particularly those of the middle class.

Middle-class Coloureds resent and fight the white stereotyping of Coloureds as drunken, apathetic, lazy, and unreliable. The middle class struggle to keep their children "respectable." They complain that the whites fail to see a class difference among Coloureds. They say, "The whites treat us as if we were all the same. Well, we're not."

Middle-class Coloureds feel the sting of the inconsistencies of *apartheid* to a greater degree than their poorer brothers. The middle class, who are "civilized" by the standards of the white government, but are still denied the rights of civilization, tend to become bitter and cynical. One Coloured man said, "You don't find us crying. We're very humorous. If you have a good job, you can afford a nice home in which to suffer in comfort." Another said, "I'll milk this system to get whatever I can, no matter what I have to say, or how I have to prostitute myself." This attitude has earned middle-class Coloureds the epithets "ass-creepers," "ass-crawlers," and "tea drinkers" from the lower-class Coloureds.

In Woodstock there is a class distinction of "above the line" and "below the line," referring to the main boulevard that bisects the community. The division is both figurative and literal. Certainly the people of upper Woodstock tend to be wealthier than those in lower Woodstock, but the primary meaning of being from above the line is that a person so described will be a "snob" who "puts on airs" and "plays white." It does not matter if a person lives in lower-lower Woodstock, he can still be accused of living above the line.

Middle-class Coloureds often do "play white," but what appears as their conspicuous consumption to the lower class may be in reality the legitimate exercise of their greater purchasing power. Certainly "ass-creeping" to whites is not the exclusive domain of middle-class Coloureds—lower-class Coloureds joke about the way they themselves adopt servile behavior in the presence of whites to gain gratuities. In summary, class differences are often on the minds of Coloureds. One printer (a high-status occupation) told me that I should visit his club "where you can meet the whole range of Coloureds from the lower to the upper class—like me."

LANGUAGE

Frantz Fanon (1968) has said, "The Negro of the Antilles will be proportionately whiter—that is, he will come closer to being a real human being—in direct ratio to his mastery of the French language." One need only substitute "Cape Coloured" for "Negro" in Fanon's sentence and "English" for "French" to have an accurate statement of the status value of language to the Coloured people. The first or home language of almost all the Cape Coloured people in Woodstock is Afrikaans. In the Cape Province, 90 percent of the Coloured people give their first language as Afrikaans. But probably all Coloured people in the Cape use Afrikaans at home, although those who consider themselves upwardly mobile often deny knowledge of Afrikaans. A Coloured often will say to a stranger, "I can't speak Afrikaans," but later, when he feels the stranger has become a friend, he will slip comfortably into fluent Afrikaans. Many Coloureds are insulted if a stranger assumes Afrikaans is their first language. Almost all Coloureds will answer a telephone and exchange greetings on the street in English. A joke in Cape Town concerns two Coloured men, neither capable of sustaining a conversation in English, babbling on incoherently for an hour because neither will swallow his pride and admit that he really speaks only Afrikaans. The joke has some basis in fact. For example, in a church in Woodstock, the parishioners voted unanimously in favor of having the pastor deliver his sermons in English. The pastor there relates that many of his parishioners later admitted to him in private that they could not understand English, but voted against Afrikaans because they did not want to lose face with their neighbors.

The general rule, according to Coloured informants, is that what is mundane, trivial, unimportant (or romantic) is spoken in Afrikaans. For example, most conversation at home is in Afrikaans. English is the language of business. To signal that one is becoming serious in his conversation, he switches to English. It is considered a great compliment if a white man addresses a Coloured in English. As Swahili was the master-servant language in upland Kenya and English the language of equals, Afrikaans has been traditionally used by whites in South Africa as the language in which orders are barked at Coloureds and insults delivered.

Because the Afrikaners are thought to be the enemy by the Coloureds and the English-speaker the liberal friend, the use of language has some political significance. Equally important, though, is the value of English in boosting the self-pride of the Coloureds. For example, there are no insulting words for Coloureds in South African English, while the expletive *Hotnot* exists in Afrikaans. In addition, a Coloured man would never be referred to as *Meneer* (Mr.) in Afrikaans. He would be called *seun* (boy) or by his first name. In compensation for this, Coloureds, even when speaking Afrikaans, address each other as "Mr." in English. Even the closest of friends will not address each other by their first names only. They will say *Goiemore, Mr. van der Stael,* and not *Goiemore, Jaime.*

The language of the Coloureds in Cape Town is a simplified version of Afrikaans (as Afrikaans is a simplified form of Dutch). Some Coloureds call their language *Gamtaal,* or Ham's language. Its most singular characteristic is the inclusion of scores of English words. This is not so unusual when one considers the number of Afrikaans words that have been adopted into South African English, but the extent of the fusing of the two languages in *Gamtaal* is extreme even for South Africa. The following poem by Coloured poet Adam Small is entitled "The Second Thanksgiving Prayer of the Skollie." The skollies are street toughs about whom more is said later. The poem is quoted first in the Coloured patois of Afrikaans, *Gamtaal,* then in English.

Djulle stywe nekke van die galoef
djulle hypocrites se heilage swanks
thanks
an' de same to you
for de season's compliments

allright ek is 'n skollie
my artificial heil ageit
is rieds by my gaborte
in symaai gaskop
die here dit self gedoen
o
hy's ganadig as hy djou
djouself lat ophou fop
so baie dankie here
thanks
for de season's compliments

* * *

You stiff necked religious types
you hypocrites and pious swanks
thanks
and the same to you
for the season's compliments

allright I am a skollie
my artificial holiness
already at my birth

was knocked to hell
the Lord did it himself
oh
he's merciful if he
helps you stop fooling yourself
so many thanks Lord
thanks
for the season's compliments

Here the language of Ham is used by a street corner Coloured boy to tell those "above the line" that "ass-creeping" and the white man's religion are merely exercises in self-delusion.

RELIGION

Religion is the most important social institution in Woodstock after the family. (The political implications of religion are discussed later.) In this section, religion is dealt with only as a criterion of class differentiation.

According to the South African Bureau of Statistics, 29.5 percent of the Coloured people are members of the Dutch Reformed Church and 17.3 percent are Anglicans. Practically no middle-class Coloureds in Woodstock are members of the D.R.C. In fact, very few inhabitants of Woodstock attend the D.R.C. Although more Coloureds are members of the D.R.C. than any other church, this membership is almost entirely rural. Sophisticated, literate Coloureds consider the D.R.C. the religious pillar of *apartheid* because only the Dutch churches practice it. (A popular story in Woodstock concerns a Coloured man who is kneeling on the floor in a D.R.C. when the parson walks in and says, "*Seun*, what are you doing here?" The Coloured man replies, "Washing the floors, if it pleases the *baas*." The parson says, "Well, that's all right. As long as you aren't praying." The story is not told to elicit laughter.) Sophisticated Coloureds find the D.R.C. particularly insidious, not only because it is actively opposed to their fondest dream of becoming part of the white group but because it denies them the last remaining aspect of social life where whites and Coloureds could meet on equal footing. For this reason, membership in the D.R.C. might vitiate any positive class status a Coloured in Woodstock might have. To the people of Woodstock, a man who is a member of the D.R.C. is either an unsophisticated farm laborer or utterly and despicably shameless. The highest-status religions are Anglicanism and Islam. Not insignificantly, these are among the least "race-conscious" religions in South Africa. Also, most wealthy Coloureds in Cape Town are either Anglicans or Moslems.

FAMILY STRUCTURE

Family structure is similarly related to class status. For example, the matrifocal family in Woodstock is mainly a lower-class phenomenon. Class status is a determining factor in the form the family will take. Middle-class, light-skinned, educated, English-speaking, Anglican Coloureds will most likely have stable, patrifocal families. The average Coloured family is poor and often matrifocal. However, the ideal pattern of family life even among poor Coloureds is the white norm.

Another coordinate of family structure, besides social rank, is the self-image of the members of the primary group, a subject discussed in the next chapter.

2 / Self-image and group image in Woodstock

To a great extent, every culture is based on myth. For a society to function smoothly its population must be socialized—people must be taught to believe in the society's myths. (To the anthropologist, "myth" is a neutral term. It refers to beliefs, to narrative, to history, whether factual or not.) In the United States, the central cultural myth is the American Dream, and the socialization of young people is based to a large extent on their assimilating this myth. Blacks believe the myth, but their self-image is destroyed when they perceive that they are unable to achieve its requirements. Since self-image, then, does not exist apart from the myths of society, myth plays an important role in both socialization and personality formation.

This interrelatedness of various parts of a social system is illustrated by the functional utility of the foundational myth of South Africa—that is, the racial superiority of whites. Coloureds, who are taught to believe the myth, experience the destruction of their self-image when they learn they can never become white. They come to believe they are inherently inferior and impure. The values and attitudes of the dominant whites are internalized by the Coloureds just as, until recently, the values and attitudes of the dominant whites in America have been largely accepted by the blacks. Myth, then, because it is central to socialization and personality formation, leaves the Coloureds socially impotent.

Social control, that powerful weapon with which men may dominate others, is another interrelated function of myth. Brute force alone could probably never keep a group of people subjugated. Often, however, a myth can accomplish this end without bloodshed. In South Africa, the Coloured people historically have been prisoners of myth.

Coloureds are taught two mythical lessons: (1) white is positive and black is negative; and, (2) racial purity is superior to mixing. These two lessons contain a seed of inconsistency. The Coloureds are forced to ask, "If white is better than black, and purity is of acknowledged value, is it better to be a little white or all black?" The dilemma is, of course, insoluble. This is as it is meant to be. For, as the first lesson establishes the superiority of whites over Africans, the second establishes the superiority of whites over the nearly white Coloureds.

The myth, by making the Coloureds as color conscious as whites, if not more so, makes them sensitive to color differences within the group. Thus they are prevented from establishing any group consciousness. The Coloureds are a people without a name. They seldom say "us" or "we." Often they refer to their own people in the third person plural. Living in a land based on the myth of race, they are in need of a myth that glorifies blending rather than purity. But there is no room for a racial melting-pot myth in a stratified nation like South Africa.

Among the Coloureds, the inconsistencies of the racial myth foster a feeling of ambivalence concerning Africans. On one hand, they subscribe to the notion that their white blood justifies their having a higher status than the Africans. In front of a Woodstock Anglican church, for example, a white priest attempted to hush his choir boys, who were shouting abuse at a passing African. "Don't worry, Father," a brown-skinned cherub reassured him, "it's only a *kaffir*." One Coloured man said to me, "Every night when we go to bed we thank God that at least we aren't black." If threat is the main cause of prejudice, as many social psychologists suggest, then the feelings of the Coloureds about Africans are understandable. The Coloureds live with the fear that their middle status will disappear and that they will be relegated to the level of the Africans. On the other hand, the Coloureds admire not only the racial purity of the Africans but their unity, strength, and stoicism. Coloureds say, "They have it worse than us, but you don't see alcoholics among them." And, "They steal from whites but Coloureds steal from Coloureds."

Another myth, referred to earlier, that causes a dilemma among the Coloureds is the myth that says every white man is *ipso facto* civilized. This equating of race with culture adds to the confusion of the Coloureds. To the Boer, a South African is one who is a Christian, shares the standards of Western civilization, speaks Afrikaans, and is white. To the Coloured, a South African is one who is a Christian, shares the standards of Western civilization, and speaks Afrikaans. The Coloureds' definition is based wholly on cultural considerations, while the Boers' includes a biological criterion. When one asks a Coloured to describe the cultural traits of his group, he will say, "They are the same as the whites'." Because they satisfy all but one of the criteria of "civilization," Coloureds cling pathetically to the white group, hoping to be admitted into European society.

In South Africa, Coloureds and whites share the same cultural symbols, yet a social disparity separates the groups. Coloureds have assimilated white views, including views of color. They are culturally indistinguishable from Europeans, but they are rejected on the grounds of color. While the nonwhite shares the values of the dominant culture that depreciates blackness, these same values exclude him from the dominant group in which he is struggling to be included. The Coloured man is thus in the inconsistent philosophical position of accepting the values of the system but not the rank that the system dictates should be his.

The Coloureds live in a world of dilemma fed by the inconsistencies of the whites. Historically, the dream of the Coloureds has been to become brown Afrikaners, but they have been rebuffed by the *laager* tendencies of the Boers. A Coloured man, in complete frustration, said, "I've done everything they've wanted me to do, but just when I think they're going to accept me, they retreat into that damn *laager*. It's made of steel. I don't think a Coloured man can penetrate it."

The important question here, of course, is why does this man want to penetrate the Afrikaner *laager*? The simple reason is that as a white man he would be far more comfortable physically than he is as a Coloured. A more complex answer is that whites constitute the reference group for the Cape Coloureds. Upwardly mobile Coloureds have so identified themselves with whites in anticipatory social-ization that they are dissatisfied with being Coloured. Most Coloureds have a white bias. Indeed, in everything but skin color they are white, yet, they are frus-trated in their attempts to become members of the white group. The sociological result of such a situation is often called marginality, the core of which is non-membership in one's reference group. The marginal man has been characterized as being excessively self- and race-conscious and harboring deep feelings of infe-riority. He is both critical of the hypocrisies of the dominant group and contemp-tuous of those subordinate to him.

It would seem that, because the status hierarchy was not entirely rigid in the past, the Coloureds were led to believe that they could become white. (Evidence of this lack of rigidity is the number of Afrikaners who are undoubtedly Col-oured.) The marginality of Coloureds stems from the fact that they were misled. It has been noted that the degree of marginality is a function of the incon-sistency between the amount of an individual's (or a group's) acculturation and the extent to which he is rejected by the dominant group. For example, al-though Africans are rejected completely by South African whites, they are not marginal men because they identify with other Africans and not whites. Except for scattered members of the urban African bourgeoisie, there are probably few Afri-cans who want to be white. The situation is quite different, however, among Col-oured people. There are many proud Zulu and Xhosa in South Africa, but it is al-most impossible for a man to be proud that he is Coloured. He may be proud of his white blood and feel superior to Africans, but this is a negative kind of pride, for the trait upon which he bases his pride is the very one that he lacks in sufficient quantity to gain admission to his reference group.

The concept of identity is implicit in many ethnographic and sociological studies. When dealing with a group, the sociologist must define it by delimiting the char-acteristics, criteria of membership, and boundaries of the group. But this delimi-tation takes place not only in the mind of the sociologist—groups themselves have yardsticks for the measurement of associational eligibility. In simple terms, all peoples have a developed sense of "we." But "we" can exist only in relation to "them." "We" have something in common that "they" do not share with us. Each individual belongs to many "we" groups. The size of the "we" group varies with the social distance of the "them" group. For example, a man and his wife are "we" in relation to the other members of their village, but all the villagers are "we" in relation to the people of the next village. Many primitive societies have a highly developed sense of hierarchy among "we" groups. Rights and obligations de-crease with each expansion of the "we" group. In all societies, some people are more "we" than others. In modern societies "we" is based first on family, then on locality, then on nation and race.

Cape Coloured people do not have a highly developed sense of "we." To Col-oureds, the only worthwhile "we" is being a member of the white group. It is as if all the Xhosa were trying to become Zulus or all Frenchmen were trying to be-come Germans. The first result would be the breakdown of order within the

Xhosa tribe and the French state. The end result would be the collapse of the Xhosa and the French as separate collectivities (with one proviso, that the Zulus and Germans were willing to accept the outsiders and grant them full membership). But the whites in South Africa are deaf to the entreaties of the Coloureds. By thus denying them membership, only the first result is obtained—there is no order or basis for group allegiance among the Coloureds. Such a situation produces a case of extreme marginality.

Groups need symbols and myths to ensure their continuing existence. Whether it be totemism or the patriotic trappings of the modern state—flag, songs, a pantheon of heroes—every successful group must have a rite or ceremony by which it celebrates its separateness. Yet, Coloured people appear to have no way to articulate their "colouredness." They continue as a group only because the whites force them to remain separate. Coloureds exist as a group only in reference to whites.

The white image of the Coloured man is the stereotype by which Coloureds judge themselves. Historically, whites have called Coloureds indolent, improvident, gregarious. Under the paternalistic system in the Cape, Coloureds have developed these traits because of their reliance on whites. It seems that white South Africans have never expected more than laziness and idleness from the Coloureds. Indeed, a white is shocked and insulted if he finds industry. Such behavior is considered "cheeky."

Through what Robert Merton (1968) calls a "self-fulfilling prophecy," Coloureds were treated as inferiors, so they adopted the behavior of inferior people. The behavior of Coloureds has been conditioned through reinforcement. The Coloured man who is servile, slow-witted, and even a bit lazy is rewarded for saying *ja, baas* and showing gratitude for everything a European does, even if he is being harmed by the action. On the other hand, a "cheeky *Hotnot*," that is, an educated Coloured or one with pride, will be punished. Because Coloureds are similar to them, whites have found it necessary to stress their inferiority, calling attention to their drunkenness, laziness, dishonesty, violence, stupidity, and immorality. Africans, on the other hand, with non-European cultures and darker skins pose less of an immediate threat to white superiority, and are thus less maligned. Where white Capetonians are not stressing the immorality and inferiority of the Coloureds, they talk about their puerility: "They're children, really," or "They're happy-go-lucky chaps." Whether the Coloured was a slave or serf, the white South African has traditionally referred to him as a "boy." Today, white South Africans look upon service jobs as natural employment for Coloureds.

Even the poor whites who live in Salt River and Woodstock, who are mainly illiterate and unskilled, treat wealthy, educated Coloureds as their inferiors. The rule is that the lowest-ranked white man must have higher status than the highest-ranked Coloured man. A recent immigrant from Greece or Portugal, unable to speak either English or Afrikaans, is immediately given higher status in the society than any Coloured man. The resentment of this practice is considerable. The Coloureds call uneducated southern European immigrants "Madeira scum"—but not to their faces. For on his first day in South Africa, the European peasant is lord over even the sophisticated nonwhite. Thus the hierarchy is maintained by reinforcing the prohibitions on Coloureds at every possible level. At work, no Coloured can ever have authority over any white. While doing the same job, he must receive a lower salary.

No matter what he does, the Coloured man cannot remove the trait of darkness that "flows in his veins." To try to vitiate the evil black traits he possesses he uses skin lighteners and hair straighteners to make him appear white. (Combs designed for hair straightening were originally imported from America, and at least one Cape Town barber learned the straightening process from American Negro hair experts.) Even the harmless clichés and idioms of European tongues seem to contain proof of the inferiority of dark peoples. Significantly, when a Coloured talks about a good child, he calls him "our blue-eyed boy" while the bad child is "the black sheep" in the family. Whatever the origins of these common European expressions, the frequency of their use and the conscious choice of using these rather than less loaded expressions are indicative of the color-consciousness of the Cape people.

The final irony for the Coloured man is that because he has internalized white attitudes toward color, he finds himself prejudiced against himself. Coloureds tend to hate other Coloureds and, therefore, themselves. For example, if a priest says he hates all priests, there must come a time when he will recognize similarities between himself and other clerics. Coloureds, using the stereotypes held by whites, call other Coloureds spineless, lazy, drunken, and oversexed. They rationalize that the whites are referring only to "other Coloureds." But the truth is that whites do not make exceptions among nonwhites—all Coloureds are thought of as Coloureds. That may sound so obvious as to appear simple-minded, but it is a truth that Coloureds, for the sake of their self-images, try to avoid. The successful or upwardly mobile Coloured tries to believe that whites will accept him. But "nonwhite" is an ascribed social status that he cannot change or even influence. The problem for the Coloured man, then, is to make his self-image agree satisfactorily with his ascribed status.

Middle-class Coloured people attempt to boost their self-esteem through avoidance mechanisms and the maintenance of a spurious "white" cultural standard. Many simply avoid the indignities of the color bar by not going to places where they would be discriminated against. One Coloured man said,

> My family just avoids going out. We'd like to go to a circus or an ice show, but you just don't feel like going when you have to sit behind a post and all you can see are the performers' backs. But when we don't go to the two or three entertainments a year where the Coloureds can attend (if they are willing to sit in miserable seats) the government says we're indifferent and the next year they make it so we can't go at all.

Middle-class Coloureds have established their own "high society" similar to that in America described by Franklin Frazier (1962) in *Black Bourgeoisie*. This Coloured bourgeoisie, composed of a very small number of light-skinned, relatively wealthy people, emulates what it perceives is the behavior of white society. The prerequisites for membership are the use of the English language and "refined" behavior. When this group gathers (usually at balls and cocktail parties) they discuss such things as the last *braai* (barbecue), their children's progress at school, and the stock market. Politics is never discussed and, according to some informants, a member would be ostracized for discussing "serious problems" (politics).

Middle-class Coloureds never acknowledge that their ancestors were slaves. They call poor Coloureds *skollies* and say of the behavior of a lower-class Coloured that it is "just like a coon." Through these varieties of self-delusion the middle-class Coloured tries to reconcile his low rank with his self-image. He must protect himself, his self-esteem, against the threats of society. To do this he must make use of certain techniques of self-defense to relieve his frustration: repression (selectively forgetting that he is not white), fantasy (playing white), ritualism (organizing a social circle where no one will remind the other of his inferiority), and rationalization (saying, "Thank God we aren't black" or, "Just look at how those other Coloureds act—you can hardly blame the whites for despising them"). Through the use of these mechanisms the conflict between low rank and the individual's strivings is partially resolved.

Even some educated, politically radical Coloureds accept the philosophy that "white makes right." A young Coloured social worker spent an hour explaining to me how evil the government was in its treatment of Coloureds. When asked how she was treated by her uneducated, white superior, she said, "Oh, Mrs. Williams is the only white person I know who isn't condescending. She even trusts us to write our own letters to the city authorities. Only occasionally will she change something. But, of course, she should know." The educated Coloured girl was, in reality, admitting that the white woman, although uneducated, had some kind of special powers because she was white. This kind of color superiority exists within the Coloured group as well. Many Coloured teachers reported that light-skinned teachers had fewer problems with discipline than their darker counterparts.

A famous example of a middle-class "Coloured" man's failure to cope with his status is the extreme case of Tsafendas, the man who killed Prime Minister Verwoerd. Tsafendas was twenty-one before he discovered that his deceased mother was an African. Until then he had accepted his darkness as not unusual for a Greek. But the discovery changed his life profoundly. Until he found out about his mother, he regarded each occasion of being asked to produce his identity card as just an ethnic joke. But afterward every challenge presented the possibility of being found out. He realized that he was not white and he became afraid of associating with whites who might question him. Therefore, he started to seek out the company of Coloureds. He fell in love with a Coloured girl but she dropped him, fearing punishment under the Immorality Act, when she found that he was classified white. Tsafendas found himself in a position where Coloureds were afraid to have him in their company, and he was too frightened to chance detection by whites. Therefore, he struck out at the man whom he probably felt was most responsible for the system and, hence, his quandary.

The facts of the Tsafendas case are murky and any analysis rests upon too much supposition to be of value in itself. It is important here, however, because of the sympathy a great many Coloureds express for Tsafendas. He represents the man without a group, a sociological situation very close to the experience of many Coloured people.

Lower-class Coloureds tend to adapt to their role through retreatist mechanisms. Because they cannot be aggressive toward whites and compliance with white norms is impossible, poor Coloureds escape through antisocial means. Typically, they use magic, gambling, drugs, and alcohol for this purpose. They quite realistically anticipate failure so they do not continue to perform the ritual of conforming to white society as middle-class Coloureds often do.

Violence is common among the poor in Woodstock because of the great percentage of Coloureds who are members of the lower class and the lack of a well-defined group identity. The first reason is self-explanatory. The second provides a key to the extensive social pathology of Woodstock. In Coloured society there is a considerable failure of social inhibitions and restraints. Every society limits violence through certain rules of conflict. Every society has prohibitions against rape, murder, assault, and theft. Such prohibitions work if individuals feel a part of the tribe or the society. But if the legitimacy of the group is not recognized, the rules will go unenforced. Coloureds do not feel a part of a legitimate Coloured society or community. There is no tight kinship system, no loyalty to race, creed, or nation. There is no ideological justification (such as societal or supernatural imperatives) for obedience to rules. The end result is that the poor, angry Coloured man moves easily to violence. In the loosely knit Coloured community there exist only loosely defined prohibitions. Since poor Coloureds have little stake in the society, there is little reason to obey its rules.

The culture of poor Coloureds is considerably different from middle-class Coloured society which emulates white standards. A perusal of either one of the two Coloured-oriented newspapers, *The Herald* and *The Post,* will give indication of this split among Coloureds. A typical headline found in one of these papers was: "13 Held after Murder Mutilation, Castrated Dad Dies at Xmas Farm Braai." Amid the advertisements for hair straighteners and skin lighteners are stories of violence (with rapes and stabbings the most popular form). Near the center of the paper there is one society page with pictures of very light-skinned Coloureds dancing and entertaining. Editorials deal with sports and other noncontroversial affairs. There is seldom any political comment, because, as is everything else that caters to Coloureds, these papers are owned by whites. Whites control all the means of influencing the self-image of Coloureds—government, communications, industry, churches, and schools. Each of these institutions continually stresses the class differences among Coloureds because the split is vital to the preservation of the racial hierarchy. The internal antagonisms among Coloureds vitiate any efforts to form a common front against the whites.

3 / Coloured families

For generations sociologists have accepted the assertion that the Negro family in the United States is more likely to be matrifocal than the white family. In South Africa, there is evidence that there are more mother-centered families among Coloured people than among whites. The causes of this situation are similar in both Watts and Woodstock. To understand these causes, it is helpful to consider the following case studies in terms of the racial hierarchy of South Africa. Economic deprivation, deflated self-image, and weak or absent fathers tend to characterize certain nonwhite families in both the United States and South Africa. The families considered below were residents of Bonteheuwel, a government housing project on the Cape sand flats.

THE KOOPMANS

Mrs. Koopman greets her visitors without getting out of bed. She calmly answers questions while her young children seem to be tearing the house down around her. She is in her thirties but looks much older. She has seven living children, five boys and two girls. Four other children died in infancy. In addition, she has had three miscarriages. She is pregnant again.

The Koopman home is a two-room blockhouse of the type called, with a certain bureaucratic flair, "subeconomic housing." It is provided by the Cape Town City Council for 4 rand per month. A toilet is shared with another equally large family. There is no running hot water and no bathtub.

Mrs. Koopman is a gregarious, talkative woman who loves to ramble on in Afrikaans patois about the inadequacies of her husband. Mr. Koopman works at the Public Works Department where he earns 8 or 9 rand a week. He recently held jobs in a toilet roll manufacturing company and a glass company. Between pregnancies, when she works as a charwoman or in local factories, Mrs. Koopman earns as much per week as her husband. Mr. Koopman seldom talks. He sits and listens to her. If he opens his mouth, she shouts, *"Hou jou blerry bek"* (hold your bloody beak). She is the *baas* of the Koopman home.

Both Koopmans were born in the country, on farms owned by Afrikaners. Mrs. Koopman never knew her father. Both went to school until standard two (about three years of schooling), then they had to quit to work. They both drifted into Cape Town as teenagers looking for jobs and excitement, met each other, had two children, then decided to marry. Mr. Koopman's father was

34

"Subeconomic" housing in the Coloured township of Bonteheuwel, one of the areas to which Woodstock residents are being removed.

against the marriage. According to Mrs. Koopman, his animosity was based on the fact that his prospective daughter-in-law's hair was too kinky.

The Koopman's first home was a wood and iron shack (a *pondokkie*) which burned down. (Mrs. Koopman proudly shows visitors the newspaper clipping about the tragedy. The article states that the fire started while she and her husband were having a fight. In a drunken stupor, it seems, Mr. Koopman knocked over a lantern.) In the early years of their marriage, Mr. Koopman used to spend practically all of his income on drink and gave his wife little for food and other household expenses. As she grew older, however, she learned how to handle him. She came under the influence of Auntie, a shebeen (speakeasy) queen and a shrewd, domineering woman. Auntie helps Mrs. Koopman balance her budget and manage her husband. "She teaches me how to be a mother," Mrs. Koopman says. Now her husband hands over his entire pay envelope to her. She gives him money for bus fare and pocket money for cigars. It seems that the change in Mr. Koopman's behavior occurred when he was unemployed and had to be supported by his wife. Apparently she extracted promises of good behavior under the threat of kicking him out into the street and letting him starve.

The daily routine at the Koopmans varies only on Saturdays and Sundays when Mr. and Mrs. Koopman get drunk together on cheap wine and brandy. It is their only form of entertainment besides gossiping with the neighbors. Mrs. Koopman attends the Baptist church on Sundays while her husband stays home with the children. Occasionally she visits her mother in the country if she has the bus fare and if her huband is sober enough to look after the children. Mrs. Koopman is a member of the Mothers' Union at the church and is a popular figure in the neighborhood. Mr. Koopman belongs to no church or clubs and apparently has no close friends. He never goes out of the house except to work and never accompanies his wife on her outings.

Mrs. Koopman can write her name, but can read only with difficulty. She likes to "read" love stories in paperback picture books which she borrows from her neighbors. Her husband prefers comic books, especially war and cowboy themes. This is their only cultural outlet. The days are otherwise filled with work, the preparing of meals, and housekeeping.

Mrs. Koopman believes she is a good mother and that she treats her children better than she was treated by her mother. She thinks, however, that it is "improper" for a mother to converse with her children. "They learn better from themselves," she says. Her oldest child is eleven. He is in sub-A grade (similar to kindergarden) at school for the fourth year. Her second child is ten and is in sub-B after having failed sub-A twice. Her seven-year-old boy was not accepted into school this year because those nearby were overcrowded.

When Mrs. Koopman goes out to shop or to work, she sends her children across the road to Auntie's or leaves them all in the care of her eleven-year-old son. She claims that her children are obedient. She realizes that she is a strict disciplinarian and is proud of the results, pointing to her eleven-year-old's responsibility in caring for the other children as proof of her success. At times her discipline can be explosive—she made one of her younger sons permanently "simple" when she held his hand over a flame for stealing five cents. However, she will not allow her husband to discipline the children because "he might injure them."

The Koopmans seldom discuss politics. Their primary complaint against the government is that they can no longer live in District Six or Woodstock where the houses are large enough for their family. Mrs. Koopman has requested a bigger house from the City Council but has not received a reply. She and her husband must sleep in the kitchen with the two youngest children. "I've seen the houses white people live in," she says. "I'd like one of those. But I'd be happy with just another room."

THE VAN WYKS

Sally van Wyk is twenty-eight years old. She lives in an unkempt three-room house with seven children by her common-law husband. He is currently incarcerated in a work colony for failure to support the family. During the interview Sally never got up from the unmade bed on which she was lying. She was wearing only a tattered, red bikini bathing suit. The children were dirty and in various stages of undress. Sally complacently let the children scream and climb all over her and the interviewer while she complained about her husband, her house, her health, the government, and the neighbors: "My husband is a pig. I hope he rots in jail. I'm better off with him there. I get 25 rand per month from the government as a maintenance grant for the children plus his salary of 4.50 rand a week from the work colony. If he gets out, I'll lose that and I'll have to feed him besides. He's a drunken lout. He gets high on *dagga* (cannabis) and brandy and beats me and the children. The bastard never works. When he first went into the colony I used to go there often just to make sure he was still safely locked in. He says he'll kill me when he gets out for having been responsible for getting him sentenced. The children are scared to death of him. To tell you the truth, I'm scared too. The neighbors love to gossip about us. Who are they to talk about other people's morals? Everybody around here is a no-good drunk. This house is a mess. Nothing I could do would make it look decent. I don't even bother trying anymore. My husband's mother comes around here and tells me what a bitch I am and how wonderful her son is. I tell her the truth about that bugger but she never listens."

Sally attended school for only one year. When she was eighteen and still living at home, she became pregnant. She started to live with the father after her first child was born. Sally could have continued to live with her mother, but she did not like her own father well enough. "Besides, if I had stayed there, I would have had to work and help support the whole family. That's not for me."

The only element of order in Sally's house are the neatly stacked piles of picture books in almost every corner of the house. "I read so many of those my eyes went bad," she says. "They gave me a pair of glasses at the hospital, but look at these ugly frames. They are so far out of fashion that I wouldn't wear them if I were going blind."

Sally has no ambitions or plans for the future. Her three oldest children, aged twelve, nine, and eight, are all in the first year of school. She has no expectations about their futures. "I just hope they grow up fast and get out on their own. I don't want to spend the rest of my life looking after them. I didn't sponge off my mother. I don't expect my kids to sponge off of me." Still, Sally visits with her mother regularly and will, in another mood, profess how close she is to her children. "It is just that there are so many of them," she says.

THE DEVRIES

Mrs. DeVries, a Moslem, was born in Cape Town forty years ago and raised in a strict Moslem family environment. She passed standard six, but her father would not allow her to continue her education beyond that point. He felt that the role of a woman was to work with her hands—not to use her mind. Mr. DeVries, a year older than his wife, was born a Christian. He was raised in a poor family that could only afford to put him through standard three. The DeVries met when she was seventeen. Her parents forbade her to see him on religious grounds. When they discovered she was pregnant by him, they disowned her.

Mrs. DeVries then went to work in a Cape Town shop and continued there for twenty-one years, taking time off only for two months at the birth of each of her ten children. When she quit last year she was making 8.75 rand per week. Mr. DeVries has been employed consistently ever since he started living with his wife. He has been an unskilled laborer all his life. Currently he works as a casual laborer on the docks. Occasionally, with overtime, he makes as much as 11.00 rand per week. Usually he earns about 9 rand.

Mrs. DeVries completely dominates her husband. She is a strong-willed, intelligent woman. He is a simple, quiet man who is treated by his wife as one of the children. After living together for sixteen years, Mr. DeVries converted to Islam and married his common-law wife in a Mosque. A few months after the wedding, Mrs. DeVries' widowed mother reconciled herself to the marriage and moved in with her daughter and son-in-law.

The ten DeVries children, aged from three months to twenty-two years, all live with their parents and grandmother in a neat three-room house. The twenty-two-year-old son is the only working child. He contributes 3.00 rand per week to the household expenses, saving the remainder of his salary for his imminent marriage. He will have to pay all the expenses of the wedding, since his fiancée's parents are as poor as his own.

When the interviewer first visited the DeVries home, he was told that Mrs. DeVries had three-month-old twins. Later, Mrs. DeVries admitted that one of the babies was her eighteen-year-old daughter's illegitimate child. Mrs. DeVries and her daughter had had babies during the same week. The daughter had at first wanted to marry the father of her child but was forbidden to do so by her own father. The father of the illegitimate child had apparently told many Moslems that Mr. DeVries was a heavy drinker, thus lowering DeVries' status in the abstemious community he had recently joined. Mr. DeVries threatened to kill the boy and his daughter if they married. Mrs. DeVries seems very proud of her husband's actions. "It was the only time he ever acted like a man in his life," she says. Now, the twenty-two-year-old DeVries son has promised to adopt his sister's child when he marries.

Mrs. DeVries says she hasn't seen her fifteen-year-old son in several months. He ran away from home because he did not want to be a Moslem. All of the other school-aged children attend the local school. The children are close to their mother. She gives them money, advice, and dispenses discipline. Mr. DeVries seldom talks to any of his children. He is a gentle man whom the children like but do not respect. He is conscientious about turning over his entire pay check to his wife, but he is seldom home except to sleep. He is "allowed" to keep his overtime earnings to spend on alcohol and tickets to "white" soccer matches.

The DeVries have no close friends. They never visit acquaintances or relatives because "there are too many children." Mr. DeVries is apolitical. His wife is interested in politics, however, and her oldest son shares his mother's antigovernment sentiments. Mrs. DeVries is critical of *apartheid* but feels the system is not entirely to blame for the poverty of the family. She feels that if her children receive education they can be economically successful in South Africa even under *apartheid*. She has no time for active political involvement. Indeed, she is not a member of any social or political organization. Her only affiliation is with the Moslem religion.

Her extrafamilial, interpersonal relationships center almost entirely around a feud she is having with her next-door neighbors, with whom the DeVries share a toilet and a water tap. She says the neighbors are "filthy swine" and she always has to "clean up their mess" in the toilet. "I asked my husband to do something about it," she says, "but he is too soft to deal with any kind of problem like that. Finally, I took the matter into my own hands. I went to the City Housing Office every day and complained until they did something about it. Now it's much better. But I still don't like living so close to those black pigs."

These three families share many problems associated with poverty—lack of education, overcrowded homes, violence, and exceptionally large numbers of children. We could expect to find these conditions in most urban slums of the world. Certain of these phenomena, however, may be intensified in rigidly stratified societies—for example, the matrifocal family structure. Sociologists have observed that in most of the societies about which we have accurate records there are two primary functional roles in a family. One is the instrumental role, which is basically economic and oriented toward the provision of food, clothing, and shelter. This role, also associated with familial management and discipline, is usually thought of as a masculine one. The other role, called the expressive, is normally feminine and is directed toward emotional patterning and social relations between family members. The person who fills this role keeps the household in order, prepares food, and cares for the children. In most families, of course, role differentiation is not clear-cut. Fathers are often concerned with emotional aspects of home life and mothers often with disciplinary duties, but it is highly unusual for one parent to be required to play both roles.

But because of economic factors that stem from the racial system of South Africa, the mother in these Woodstock families is both the instrumental and the expressive leader of the household, while the father is only a marginal member. The mother, in each case, earns a large share of the family income. Generally, matrilineal bonds are stressed over the patrilineal. This is, of course, not true in all Coloured families, but it is far more common among poor Coloureds than among any other group in South Africa. In the majority of poor Coloured families the woman probably disciplines the children, is often the family breadwinner, invariably handles the family finances, and tends to be the acknowledged "boss" in the family. Although matrifocality is common in poor families, it is somewhat ameliorated when a man can earn enough to support his family without his wife's earnings. There appears to be a correlation between the husband's economic position and whether the mother or father line is stressed in the family. For example, true matrifocality, in which the household consisted of grandmother, mother, and her children, was found only in instances of extreme poverty and deprivation.

The families presented in the case studies above are fairly representative of poor Coloured Capetonians. There are exceptional families who are worse off economically than these and others who are more comfortable. For example, I visited one family of thirteen children and two adults, all living in a one-room tin and clapboard shanty without electricity, running water, or sanitary facilities. The parents were deaf and dumb and their children stole or earned food for the group. Every member of the family was covered with flies and other insects and most of the younger children were naked. At the other extreme was a Coloured man and wife who lived in a new twelve-room house with their two children. Neither of these cases is in any way typical. Most urban Coloureds are born into an environment of casual sex, alcohol, drugs, crime, and violence, but most, at least, live in separate sturdy homes and can find employment often enough to stave off starvation.

But for all classes the social system of South Africa places a low value on Coloured people and seriously diminishes their chances in life and restricts their lifestyles. Therefore, mothers, fathers, and children in Woodstock are forced to behave in ways different than their white counterparts. Family roles in Woodstock are unsatisfying to those who play them, for the Coloured people are handicapped in their desire to meet role expectations set by white standards. It is difficult to be a father if society does not recognize one as a man. It is likewise difficult to be a successful mother without a successful husband. Children, who learn their family roles from their parents, are brought up on the lesson of failure.

COLOURED MOTHERS

This discussion of family roles in Woodstock begins with the most important figure, the mother. If an old woman in a primitive society is asked to retell her life story, she will often divide her life into clearly delimited periods. She may recount her youth as a carefree time of playing with her age mates. She may recall proudly her initiation into her society. Then she will discuss her betrothal and marriage and the festivities that accompanied these occurrences. Most old women in modern societies are able to recall summer vacations, school chums, wedding ceremonies, and baby showers. The life of the Coloured woman, however, is bereft of "occasions." An old Coloured woman cannot talk about the dramatic events of her life as a woman in a primitive society can, nor can she recall the excitement and discovery of adolescence as can a woman in a modern Western culture. To the poor Coloured woman, life is uneventful toil. To some extent her childhood is a carefree time, as it is to little girls everywhere; but for the poor Coloured woman it is punctuated by periods of hunger, experiences of violence, and, perhaps, desertion by her father. There are no birthday parties, pink dresses, or visits to the department store to see Father Christmas. Her short school years will be remembered for her mother's struggle to pay for her books and clothes. As soon as she is able to care for herself she will be given the responsibility of looking after her younger brothers and sisters. Shortly after puberty she will probably lose her virginity to a boy she scarcely knows, most likely on the garbage-filled open scrubland of the Cape's sand flats—in the cold, without contraceptives, and only a piece of cardboard for a bed. If she is lucky, she will not become pregnant until she is fifteen or sixteen. She may bear one or two children in her mother's house before she establishes a household of her own with a man who may or may not be the father of her children, who may or may not marry her, and who probably will not be able to fully support her.

The strength of the wife role in poor Coloured society lies in the fact that a woman can always fulfill her feminine functions as homemaker and mother, while it is not always possible for a man to fulfill his masculine function as a breadwinner. In Woodstock, a Coloured woman can obtain a fairly well-paying job in the garment industry even if she has had less than six years of education, or she can always find a steady job as a domestic without having attended any school. The income that can be provided by a Coloured man is seldom sufficient to support a family. It falls upon the mother both to make the home *and* to supplement family income. This strengthens her position in the family and increases its general female bias, as the following case illustrates.

The Hertzogs live in Woodstock. They have been married for a year and have two children. (Mrs. Hertzog gave birth to their first child while still living with her mother.) Mr. Hertzog has never been steady in his work habits. When he does work, he earns nearly 12 rand a week as a city street sweeper. Mrs. Hertzog works regularly as a domestic and earns 11 rand a week. Mrs. Hertzog's mother moved in with the Hertzogs when her husband died. She quickly established herself as the head of her daughter's household. Her fights with Hertzog are loud and violent. He is absent from home for long periods of time on alcohol and *dagga* binges. Once, when drunk, he rushed into the house brandishing a knife and threatened to kill his mother-in-law. He was restrained by his wife and several neighbors. Hertzog calls his wife's mother Hitler and rhetorically asks what right she has to boss him around in his own house. Mrs. Hertzog and her mother do not need to answer his question. They pay the rent and have purchased all the furniture and household goods with their own money. Their positions are far more secure than Hertzog's.

In 1960, 2,285 Coloured men were convicted of failure to support their children, a conviction rate six times that among whites in South Africa. For the Coloured man, the way of least resistance points to the streets and obliteration of his failures in *dagga*, brandy, and reassuring camaraderie. Both a cause and effect of his desertion is the strength of the wife. To a young Coloured man, a woman is a distant, lurking creature waiting to trap him, to engulf him, unless she is seduced, taken violently and quickly, and abandoned. Marriage is not a state that a young man anticipates with pleasure. It is a hazard that befalls the unlucky. After marriage the attitude changes little. The state of matrimony is rarely considered permanent—it is entered because it provides a place to live (single men cannot obtain public council housing), steady sex, and hot meals. Some men who marry do not consider the state to be a lifelong commitment. If the marriage is bad, a man will readily exchange it for a better, or at least a new, situation. Women realize this and buttress themselves in anticipation of desertion. If desertion occurs, mother and child will often go to live with the mother's mother or, less commonly, with one of the mother's sisters. (The confusion this situation causes in the minds of children cannot be discounted. A child raised in his grandmother's home, where his mother is also a dependent of the grandmother, will probably develop a considerable degree of social ambiguity toward female roles.)

Many Coloureds say that it is a mark of respect for married women to visit their mothers and that mothers should never visit their daughters. The basis of this custom could be that a married woman really never leaves home permanently. She knows that she can always return to the home of her mother in case of difficulty. Visiting "home" in Woodstock is a literal exercise among married Coloured women because home is the wife's mother's residence, not her conjugal household. Some informants claim that in Woodstock women have many children as a form of social insurance. Women are said to reason that a few of their children (particularly the sons) will leave them, never to be seen again, that a few will die before middle age, but that one or two will help to support Mamma in her old age. A poor Coloured woman in her fifties is in the most secure time of her life. She has one or two of her children contributing to her welfare and may also have a pregnant daughter living at home who is receiving a maintenance grant and thus contributing to the family coffer. Most important, she has reached menopause and no longer has to worry about pregnancies and the insecure dependency on a man coincident to that state.

There are other secure female roles in Woodstock besides that of grandmother. One is the shebeen queen, who may employ three or four men in her illegal business. She has what is undoubtedly the highest-paying profession a Coloured woman can have. For many reasons her status in the community is exceptionally high (for one, she is in a position to grant credit toward the purchase of alcohol). Because of her economic power, her status in her home may be practically that of an autocrat, for she is in no way reliant upon a man. Her man or men rely upon her. Another high-status job for a Coloured woman is that of midwife. As most poor Coloured children are not born in a hospital, the midwife is a busy, important person in the community. Because of her skills, she holds a respected position in the community with consequent strength in her family.

To understand why a woman with a steady income has such high status in her community, one need only consider how her position appears to the woman who is not self-sufficient and must rely on her husband for her livelihood. In such cases the economy of the home cannot be planned because the income and expenditure of the man are irregular—unlike the steady income that an employed woman can provide. When the man is the chief provider there is a tendency toward periods of scarcity. A mother in this situation, who can give her children only black coffee and bread for breakfast and corn meal or rice with a small piece of fish for dinner, will view with envy the self-sufficient woman who can feed her children three nourishing meals a day.

COLOURED MEN

The poor women of Woodstock play instrumental family roles because of their relatively favored social and economic position in South African society as compared with their men. The latter become drop-outs from their families and society, withdrawing in order to avoid potential conflict situations.

When a Coloured man hears an Afrikaner shout *Booi!* he reflexively turns to see if he is the "boy" who is being called. The Coloured man has been carefully and expertly taught to jump when the "master" says jump. He calls all white men "master" in English or *baas* in Afrikaans. Such deferential behavior is rewarded negatively. If the Coloured man behaves as he should, he is not always recompensed, but if he behaves in a way that displeases *die baas*, he is invariably punished. For this reason the Coloured man is punctilious in his deference to whites. He behaves in accordance with all the rules of servility down to the last rite of turning his eyes from the master when he is being castigated. The Coloured man learns that he will not be rewarded for hard work or enterprise, but will be punished if he is not self-debasing and does not conform to the protocol of the master–servant relationship. One must view the reproachable and otiose behavior of Coloured men in light of their social training. (It is very important to stress that I am generalizing about the poorest coloured men only in this section.)

Coloured men are weak fathers by their own standards. It is difficult for a man to be servile in one context and masterful in the next. The self-demeaning role Coloured men are bound to play in society is too demanding to allow them to step out of the role in their homes. Only the most facile of actors could play two radically divergent parts simultaneously, and most Coloured men are not good actors. They learn their role so thoroughly that they come to believe that it is their real selves. Their servile behavior becomes genuine servility.

Very young Coloured boys play cricket on the streets of Woodstock and dream of representing South Africa in a test match against England. Few adolescent Coloured boys play cricket, however, because they know that they cannot step upon the lush cricket fields of Cape Town except as gardeners. They have learned the lesson that the swings in the park are not for them, that the well-kept soccer field is forbidden to nonwhites, and that youth itself appears to be reserved for whites only. By adolescence, the Coloured boy has forgone the dreams of cricket in favor of the real world of knives, gangs, *dagga*, and theft. Once the Coloured boy learns that the fantasies of youth cannot be realized by inferior peoples, he sets out to prove his worth in ways other than sport.

Poor Coloured men become withdrawn at an early age. They often have little communication with their mothers and fathers and are dragged into maturity by the other boys in the street. There, communication is exciting: sex, liquor, and crime. In Woodstock, the sexes play separately from an early age. Mothers try to keep their daughters in the home and off the streets for as long as possible. Therefore, without girls, Cape Town Coloured boys are said often to have homosexual first experiences. For most boys such activity wanes as the girls start to break away from their mothers, but for some—probably those from exaggerated matriarchal homes—homosexuality becomes a livelihood if not a way of life.

By enforcing the law that makes sexual intercourse between a man and a woman of different races illegal, and by punishing the white men as severely as the Coloured women, South African authorities have nearly eradicated Coloured prostitution in Cape Town. The law makes no mention of homosexual activity, however, so where there was once a busy trade in the flesh of Coloured women, there was in 1968, in its stead, a market for Coloured men. Even the most masculine gang members may allow themselves to be picked up by white men. They rationalize their actions by saying that they do not enjoy the activity and do it only to make money. In Woodstock there is also a tradition of institutionalized transvestism. These transvestites, called *moffies,* are established figures on the streets of District Six and Woodstock. According to older informants, they were once quite numerous and catered as much to Coloured men as to whites. Some are reputedly quite wealthy and it is said that a few support young *skollies.*

Continued homosexual activity is only for those who have given up the struggle to remain masculine in an environment hostile to nonwhite masculinity. Most Coloured men compensate for this hostility by becoming overtly masculine. Sex conquest is one of the few ways in which a poor Coloured man can prove his masculinity: He can boast among his peers of the ways he manipulates women. A common expression is, "I used thoughts to have her." In other words, exploitation is a sign of intelligence. To outsmart a woman is a great, honorable feat.

It is only among his male friends that the Coloured man can forget his inferiority. His friends, unlike his dominant wife, present no challenge to him. They too are dark-complexioned, defeated males. Among them a jovial conversationalist has high status. Being a "good fellow" in the eyes of one's peers is the highest status one can achieve in a society where wages and other methods of upward mobility are restricted by legal and conventional color bars. With his friends, the Coloured man drowns his failures in alcohol.

Marriage takes the Coloured man away from his friends in the street and into a situation where he is constantly reminded of his worthlessness. Due to overcrowding and strained marital relations, it is impossible for him to entertain his friends at home. Thus, in marriage, he becomes isolated. He must face alone his failures to provide a decent home for his family. In the family, frustration with his role increases. His hungry children are proof that he is unsuccessful both as a father and as a man. Without membership in a social group, without any identification with his race, without even the support of his unstructured peer group, he must accept all failures personally. He has no importance in society and he is of little value in his home. His wife makes the decisions, disciplines the children, and makes all major purchases. He contributes a share of the money to meet expenses and has sexual rights. But this is the extent of his role. His children will not inherit anything of value from him. They do not acquire membership in any social group by virtue of their relationship to him. Because there is little occupational differentiation among poor Coloured men, the social status of his family is not defined by his occupational status, as is the case among whites. A special relationship between father and son is absent because there is little that the father can do for the son. The poor Coloured father cannot pass on his trade, fortune, or family history to his son. All he has is his name and this is of negligible utility to his child. As in other matrifocal societies, the father in Woodstock is of marginal social value to his children as a progenitor.

In Woodstock, the roles of mother, sister, maternal grandmother, and maternal aunt are of more importance then parallel paternal roles. The father's authority and the influence of his descent line are not developed. There is no reason for his children to look upon him as an important member of the family group. His presence is of little significance socially or economically. No matter how the Coloured father attempts to exert himself in the family, he is still unable to establish his importance. To do so, he would have to make himself a respected member of the larger social system. He would first have to secure skills, a good job, and self-esteem. Since he cannot accomplish these things, he may manifest his frustration through drinking, quitting the job he has, abdicating the little family responsibility that is his, and rejoining his friends on the street. This giving up of the struggle is the result of what could be called a Sisyphus syndrome. It is expressed by the words, "No matter what I do, I just can't make it."

Desertion among Coloured men is usually not permanent, as it often is among black Americans. The Coloured man will characteristically spend most of his time on the street and come home only when there is nothing else to do (in which case, of course, the wife may not accept him back into the house). Desertion among Coloureds often takes the form of dereliction of duty, as the following case indicates:

> Jaime Koch says that he refuses to work because his wife, Rose, would use his wages to support her mother and sister. Jaime has, therefore, relied on his wife for economic support since they started living together six years ago. They have seven children. Rose's sister, who lives with the Kochs, watches the children while Rose works. Rose is a factory worker who has been employed since she was fifteen years old. Since the Kochs began cohabiting, Jaime has been in jail on numerous occasions for drunkenness, theft, and failure to support their children. Yet, he is one of the most popular men on the street. His comrades say that he is "tough," "cool," "a good bloke," and a successful "lover." According to his sister-in-law, Jaime has had sexual relations with his oldest daughter. Jaime

does not attempt to deny her accusation. When his wife and sister-in-law start to criticize him, he ignores them and calmly walks out of the house. Occasionally, he stays away for as long as a week at a time.

Jaime Koch is a member of the lower class. It would be unusual to find fathers like him in middle-class Coloured families. The economically more secure middle-class families tend to have greater stability than poorer families because of the higher position of the husband-father in the general social system. Yet, even among the professional classes, one finds that family structure is affected by the social milieu in which it exists. It seems that the poorer Coloured people feel more acutely the effects of social and economic discrimination than do the middle classes; but no matter how wealthy a Coloured family is, it probably can never shield itself entirely from the effects of *apartheid*. The following case study of a Coloured father, who possesses all of the usually accepted criteria for middle-class standing, demonstrates the way family life among the wealthier and the better-educated Coloureds is at least partially a product of the South African social system:

Edmund is a twenty-seven-year-old schoolteacher. He has "white" features and brown skin. He is from a middle-class family that claims German mission-ary ancestry. Edmund speaks English without a South African accent, yet his home language is Afrikaans. He is very close to his widowed mother (she had been divorced for many years before Edmund's father died, however) and to his oldest sister. His mother lives with his sister, her husband, and their two children in a new, neatly furnished home. Edmund's sister is a midwife with a high, steady income. Her husband, Bill, is a truck driver and a marginal family member. His children look to Edmund as the "father" of the family. Bill is not consulted in family matters and generally takes a passive role in relation to his mother-in-law, wife, and brother-in-law. He is called on to do tasks considered too heavy or onerous for the rest of the family. Edmund calls his sister's children "my little girls" and spends hours playing with them in a fatherly fashion while Bill works or sits by uncomfortably. Even though Edmund is in a domi-nant family position compared with Bill, he is subordinate to his sister and particularly to his mother, who is the unchallenged authority in the family.

Although Edmund is very much a part of this maternal family, he lives alone in a small, deteriorated house in Woodstock. He spends most of his free time sulking and drinking. He sees no future for himself in South Africa, but does not have high enough qualifications to secure a teaching post in Britain or Canada. He is not a political activist, although he has been investigated by the South African secret police for seditious behavior. (He had told his thirteen-year-old students to call whites Mr. rather than use the customary term, *baas*. He was warned that he would be watched, but he was not taken to court.) Edmund thinks of himself as a white man and cannot reconcile himself to the servile behavior expected of him in the society. He says, "The government tells the so-called Coloureds that Africans are dangerous beasts and that they're better than the kaffirs. Then they tell the Africans, 'You're pure, whites are pure, but what the hell is a Coloured?' Color is everything in this society. My sisters are more successful than I am because they're lighter . . . Although I can sometimes pass for an Afrikaner, there are Coloureds who won't associate with me because they think I'm black. But I'm not black. I've tried to make friends with Africans, but to them I'm white. They won't even talk to me. . . . I hate whites. The lowest thing a Coloured man can be is an ass-crawler, one who says *ja, baas* while the white man insults him. . . . I'm as good as a white man. I speak their languages better than they do. . . . But violence isn't the answer. Even if the Africans take over, this will still be a racialist society."

All of Edmund's best friends are white. His only close Coloured friends are girls. He has slept with several white girls, however, a fact about which he proudly boasts. Edmund describes people by their color in such a way that the outsider who is not color-conscious has difficulty in following his portrayals. He describes one of his nieces as the "black one" and the other as the "white one." To a non-South African they both appear about the same shade of light brown.

Before Edmund will meet with a white bureaucrat he will often become very drunk. He will start such a meeting by being polite, but soon he will perceive insults in the behavior of the white official that will elicit a flow of invectives from Edmund—cut off only when he barges out of the office, his business left incomplete.

Edmund says, "I don't worry about *apartheid*; I go where I wish." In fact, he does not. However, he will often attempt to break through barriers of customary segregation, such as going to public places where nonwhites would normally be present only as servants. But his protests are ineffectual. He will come away from such an encounter in a furious rage, saying, "Did you see how those people looked at me? I could have poked their eyes out."

Edmund lives in a world between dream and reality. He wants to be white, tries to be white, and hates himself when he fails. He dislikes "ass-crawlers" and fears violence. He dreams of a quick overthrow of the system that would instantly transform South Africa into a prejudice-free land where all men are equal. But when he realizes that he is doomed to a role of inferiority he cannot accept, he says, "I hate my blackness. I can't look in a mirror." During these periods he retreats into a world of alcohol and drugs.

Edmund says that the only girl he ever wanted to marry was a white girl he knew casually. He is the father of an infant child by his long-time Coloured girl friend, Betsy. He refuses to marry her on the grounds that his mother says she is "too dark" for him (in fact, she is lighter than Edmund). The truth of their estrangement probably lies in the fact that Betsy is a typically strong Coloured woman, much like Edmund's mother. But Edmund's ideal is a soft, passive white woman. But the difficulty may even be deeper than this, in the region where color and sex conflict in stratified societies. Edmund describes his antipathetic condition: "I love Betsy, but I can't marry her. She's the mother of my child, she says. But I can't be too sure. You see, she was light enough to go out with white men and not get arrested. It seemed she was with a different one every night. She said she didn't like them but was just using them. They gave her clothes and jewels. I hated that. When she was finished with them, she would come home to see me with the gifts the white men would give her. She expected me to be proud of them because they were gifts from 'white men.' She couldn't understand when this would infuriate me. That's why I can't marry her. What if the child was one of theirs?"

It is in the home that Coloured children learn that they are inferior beings. In the home, Woodstock's children come to hate their fathers for their feckless indifference and their mothers for their unfeminine dominance. At home, Coloured children learn to hate Coloured people. Amid violence, crime, and indiscriminate sex they learn what it is to be one of the children of Ham. Young Coloured girls learn from their fathers that men cannot be trusted, and young Coloured boys learn from their mothers that women are cold and powerful:

Anne is a light-skinned twenty-five-year-old school teacher. She lives with another Coloured girl of the same age. Neither has dated a Coloured man for several years. Anne says, "I could never marry a Coloured man, they're so spineless. If I decide to marry, I guess I'll have to leave the country to find a man. My roommate may go to Botswana to marry an English missionary. The only Coloured men who are even slightly masculine are Moslems, but most of them are worthless too. . . . My father was a very dark man, but very strong for a Coloured, yet my mother bossed him about. She is very light. One day when they were driving around Johannesburg, the police stopped them. They thought she was a white woman with an African. They beat my father and dragged my mother from the car, calling her a whore and worse. . . . My father had a small shop in a Coloured neighborhood. Some local thugs robbed him and killed him in front of my ten-year-old brother. The little boy has never been the same since. Sometimes my mother locks him in the closet because he's so strange, and she is too lazy to care for him properly. . . . She drank up all of our inheritance and married a white man. That's about all you can expect from a Coloured person, I guess. It makes me sick to think about what the whites have made of us."

A common expression among Coloureds, used when a man is knifed, a woman is raped, or a store is robbed, is, "What can you expect from bastards?" A Coloured boy was asked to explain why he had knifed a *babbie* (an Indian shopkeeper). He shrugged his shoulders and replied, "I was born a bastard." The quality of bastardy is essential to any explanation of the social life of the Cape Coloured people. What it means to be a bastard, an inferior man, is the most important lesson the Coloured child learns. Bastardy is very nearly the only element of cultural folklore that the Coloured people have. Stompie, a pseudonym of a Coloured humorist, explains why January first should be declared a holiday for Coloured people:

Now, Jan van Riebeeck [Dutch explorer of the Cape] did mos [in fact] land here early in April, hey? According [therefore] van Riebeeck Day. So de firs' t'ing dose Hollanders does when dey lands are to pallie up to de Hottentot girlies in de superminiskirtjies. Dose girlies had minis and topless an' de whole boksemdice [kit]. An' you know mos' dose Hollanders been on de watter a blerrie [bloody] long time. . . .

So okay, you count nine months from de beginning of April, an' see where you comes out. Right! Beginning of Jannewarre. Nuwejaar. Tweede Nuwejaar [second of January]. Dere was so many dat dey did somma' call de ouens [fellows] according de calendar. Dat's why dere is so many Jannewaries and Febbewaries among de Coloured people.

So dat de special meaning of Nuwejaar are dat it are really de time of de birth of de Coloured People. Dat's why de Coloured People did always have a special feast time dose days. [New Year's is the most important holiday to the Coloureds. It is the time of the Coon Carnival.]

. . . We got to start a compaign. Like de Afrikaner. He are always starting campaigns. Now we start a birthday campaign.

We collecks money to build a monument. Somma here, byre Castle Bridge, byre start of District Six. An' we puts a plate on which read:

Here (or very nearby) de firs' Coloured Person were born on Nuwejaar (or very near) in 1653.

4 / Preriot Watts

At the turn of the century several hundred blacks lived in rural squalor in what was called Mudtown, eight miles south of Los Angeles. Mudtown was a generic name for the settlements of shacks and shanties erected by black migrants near many northern cities. Officially, Los Angeles' Mudtown was called Furlough Track and occupied the space between two railroad rights of way. The houses in Furlough Track were built of tar paper tacked on surplus wooden planks. The area experienced a small migratory wave of blacks from the South during World War I, and the black population soon spilled over into adjoining Watts, the home of a few thousand European immigrants. In the 1920s Los Angeles experienced a boom in oil, movies, airplanes, and oranges. The city spread south, and Watts was annexed in 1926.

A steady stream of migrant blacks during the next fifteen years was practically lost amid an even greater influx of whites into the sun-parched region of southern California. But the greatest black migration to the West was still to come. World War II attracted over one hundred thousand blacks to man the aircraft factories of the Golden State, a land of opportunity for the educated and the skilled. But few migrant Negroes could claim these qualifications when competing with whites for jobs. When white workers returned home from the war, the blacks started losing their jobs. By the economic recession of the 1950s, the unemployment rate for blacks in Los Angeles was probably as high as that for blacks in the South. But the sun, freedom, and the myth of opportunity continued to give impetus to the great migration—until the riot of 1965 finally slowed the constant stream of those searching for the good life.

Although few blacks found a promised land in southern California, most migrants decided to stay. Neither the schools nor health and welfare services were satisfactory, but they were better than those in the South. The police did not always treat blacks with respect, but there was little real physical violence done to blacks by whites—a constant possibility in the South. Watts was no Zion of employment, but at least it was warm enough so that no one froze while standing in line in winter at the state bureau of employment. There was little organized crime in Watts, at least not on the scale of Harlem or the Chicago ghetto. Physically, at any rate, the black man was better off in Los Angeles than he would have been anywhere else in America, so he stayed. He was bored, frustrated, restless, and disillusioned, but *faute de mieux*, he knew this was the place where he would grow old and die.

But the black man left something behind when he left the South. No matter how bad the South was, it was still home. A man knew where he stood in the South and, abject as his rank may have been, he found there a sense of surety and community.[1] There was no doubt in his mind as to where he stood with whites, the police, his own black community, his kin. But whether he came straight to Los Angeles from a rural area or migrated by stages, stopping first for a few years in a southern town, the transition to life in what is undoubtedly the most modern city in the world was often too abrupt for the black migrant. Having cast aside the family bonds and religious restraints of his home, he floundered. Drunkenness, crime, drugs, family disorganization, prostitution, and juvenile delinquency almost invariably develop among people with a folk culture when they are set adrift in urban areas. Men become tribeless, alone in what Franklin Frazier called the "City of Destruction."

The most dramatic result of this migration was its destructive effect on family life. Eleven percent of rural (mainly southern) black families in the United States were headed by females in 1965. In Watts, the figure was close to 40 percent. The migrant was driven by poverty, ignorance, and racial segregation into slum areas where most institutions of life as he knew them had disappeared. The tension caused by relocation was aggravated by individuals being freed from the sanctions of their natal society at exactly the moment these restraints would have been of most comfort and support. The problem was compounded by the black man's difficulty in adjusting to a kind of economy different from that he knew in the South. A great many of the people migrating to Watts could have been considered peasants trying to adjust overnight to what was for them an industrial revolution.

Frazier (1948) first noted a correlation between family problems, migration, and unemployment among blacks in the 1930s. Similarly, in Watts during the 1950s and 1960s, migrant families tended to have higher rates of unemployment, illegitimacy, juvenile delinquency, and other manifestations of family disorganization. The root cause of this complementary relationship appears to have been that

---

[1] In contrast to the weak kinship bonds found among blacks in Los Angeles, most of the migrants retained strong ties with their families in the South. Partly this was "old country" idealization, no doubt, but one heard about the "folks back home" too often for the ties to have been pure fiction. Strong emotional bonds also linked the black Los Angelenos to the South. One often found Louisiana-born blacks congregating in one place. Each southern state group claimed unique cultural peculiarities—food, language, and manners. Signs on Watts restaurants read: "Mississippi Soul Food" or "Louisiana Cookin'."

A few ghetto residents' taste ran to even more exotic southern-style delicacies than "gumbo and greens." Some blacks imported and consumed a variety of Dixie clay called "Mississippi Mud." Impossible to acquire in California, the mud was mailed to Watts from friends in the South. Another southern habit was the consumption—particularly by pregnant women —of laundry starch. This food substitute is not related to hunger. It is a southern habit analogous to chewing tobacco. Both clay and starch compete with iron in the blood and, if enough is consumed, can lead to an easily cured case of anemia. Three or four cases a week of clay- or starch-caused anemia were reported at Los Angeles County Hospital in 1967. Although starch consumption was an infrequent and unusual instance of a cultural link with the South, it is accurate to say that culturally and psychologically, "home" was below the Mason-Dixon line for almost all migrant blacks.

the southern male migrant in Watts was unskilled and uneducated, therefore unable to find a job to support his family.

Migration and unemployment were highly correlative factors in Watts in the 1960s, but even those migrants fortunate enough to secure employment still found themselves in a disadvantageous economic position. To make ends meet, the wife was forced to seek employment or welfare. When the poor black migrant's dreams of a new Jerusalem was dashed on the rocks of unemployment, when his wife could support his family and he could not, when he suffered such powerful blows to his self-esteem that he had to prove his manhood through drink, womanizing, and crime, he was effectively socialized to the role of "nigger."

As the children of Ham in South Africa adopted the behavior of social inferiors, the black migrant in Watts did likewise. Migration into Watts perhaps had begun to slow prior to the riots, but the problems of identity were reinforced by a continuing socialization process that stressed the inferiority of blacks. Some classes of black people were in the economic position to shelter themselves from this pervasive group denigration, but their numbers were small.

CLASS STRUCTURE

Most early sociologists who dealt with black communities noted at length the class differences that existed among Negroes. The class fissure was illustrated by an apocryphal middle-class Negro epithet, "those other niggers," which was applied to all black people who did not comply with Ego's standards (which Ego believed were also white standards). Certainly, among black Los Angelenos there was a status hierarchy based on life-styles, income, education, family structure, and color. Middle-class blacks tended to have more stable families and to take more of an active interest in community and civic affairs than did lower-class blacks. On the whole, as sociologists found in other black communities, middle-class social and family institutions in Watts more closely approached the white norm than did those found among the lower class.

More important than class differences in Watts, however, were the differences between white and black. The role of "nigger" was not confined solely to the lower class, as most sociologists would have had us believe. Middle-class blacks may have called the lower class "niggers" and the lower class may have called the middle class "Uncle Toms," but in American society (where all members of one race were grouped together by the dominant whites), class differences within the subordinate group did not necessarily signal differentiation of treatment. The end result of whites lumping all blacks together in one denigrated category was that many black customs and institutions crossed all class lines. The black bourgeoisie could not escape the denigrating influences of "niggerdom" by being accepted into the ranks of the whites.

In Watts, the people talked of "low-riders" who were the "brothers," the poor, the destitute, the lower class. Like the people of Woodstock who divide their community above and below the "line," the poor people of Watts divided black Los Angeles in half, symbolically, at Central Avenue. An "east-sider" was a "low-rider," a poor black, a "brother." A "west-sider" was a middle-class Negro, one who had little sympathy for poor blacks, a "white man's nigger," a "house nigger," an Uncle Tom. It was not considered relevant that nearly as many poor blacks lived on the west side of town, or that one could find Uncle Toms a mile east of Central Avenue, because class was not a fixed notion to the people of Watts—it was a transitory state of mind. Class structure in Watts was so dynamic that a sociologist treads on shifting ice when he attempts to describe literally what was essentially abstract in design. Although class standing usually correlated with income, education, and so on, this was not necessarily so. A poor black man who "put on airs" or "acted white" could have been called a west-sider, an Uncle Tom, or middle class. Similarly, a wealthy Negro who "acted black" could have been considered a brother, an east-sider, perhaps even a low-rider. (The term "lower-class" would have been used only by a west-sider as a derogatory reference, as in "those lower-class people.") Although these distinctions existed, class in black Los Angeles, as in Cape Town, was not a clear-cut issue.

In a futile effort to ascribe rank among blacks, most sociologists have failed to emphasize the factors that unite blacks as well as those that divide them. Until recently, in America, a rich or a poor black, be he a low-rider or an Uncle Tom, was, in the final analysis, a "nigger" in a system of racial stratification that tended to group all blacks together irrespective of class.

The point to be brought forward here is that even though class differences were real and deep in Watts, there were certain traits related to self-esteem that all blacks shared regardless of class. The social system of the United States assured that *all* classes of blacks idealized white standards of beauty and success. In all classes, black women were in a more favorable social and economic position than black men. In all classes, black women tended to have more power in their families than did equivalently situated white women in their families. Although manifesting the phenomenon in different ways, all classes of blacks, particularly men, suffered from denigrated self-esteem.

Certainly, the majority of black families in Watts were stable, the majority of black men were not unemployed migrants, the majority of blacks may not have been living in poverty, the majority of people were not alcoholics, drug addicts, prostitutes, or thieves, but almost all blacks were socialized to the role of "nigger." Whether it be the role of "middle-class nigger" or "lower-class nigger" was not always of great consequence in light of the overwhelming aspect of inferiority that was built into the role.

In 1965, there were 2,890 employed men in Watts. Only 290 of these men had middle-class status jobs (professional, technical, clerical, sales). In the same year, 1,840 women were employed in Watts, 390 in middle-class status jobs. The median income of a family in Watts in 1965 was $3,771—about half that of whites in Los Angeles. From these figures one can deduce that only a fraction of the people of Watts were economically middle class. The percentage of middle-class blacks increased greatly, however, if one moved out of the ghetto core and included the county as a whole.

Watts, then, was a predominantly lower-economic-class community. But, most significantly, economic class was not a wholly reliable predictor of family structure or self-esteem. This singularly important finding helps us to understand why middle-class blacks joined their poor brothers after the riots in an attempt to create a black nationalism in Watts. The reason for middle-class disaffection was, as already mentioned, primarily the social system of America that made little allowance for the class of the black man. The society denigrated him no matter what his occupation or income. Equally important, the economic position of the middle-class black *vis-à-vis* the middle-class white was proportionately less favorable than that of the lower-class black as compared to the lower-class white. Before the riots, the black with only a primary school education earned 61 percent of the lifetime salary of a similarly situated white. The black with a university degree earned only 53 percent of the salary of the white college graduate. This inequality indicates the diminishing value of higher educational achievement for blacks.

Thus, middle-class blacks, much as those in the lower class, experienced employment difficulties that struck at their self-esteem. The middle-class man was probably even more vulnerable to depressed self-esteem than the lower-class man because he could get closer to success—he could acquire all the credentials and prerequisites—but he could never quite achieve success in the way the white man could. The middle-class black was more likely to be reminded daily of his blackness through his constant contact with whites. In the heart of Watts, there were poor blacks who never met any whites except policemen and never saw any others except on television. But the higher the status of a black, the more frequent and intimate his contact with whites.

Wealth could not shield an individual in a pervasive system of discrimination. For instance, middle-class blacks showed a far higher rate of family disorganization than middle-class whites. Although blacks in the highest social classes tended to have more stable families than poor blacks, they still fell far behind the white norm. Figures from the 1960 census show that, based upon the percentage of fathers absent from the home, upper-class black families were nearly as disorganized as lower-class white families. And these statistics do not indicate whether the black men present in the homes were in fact the leaders of their families. Observation in black Los Angeles revealed a strong matrifocal bias in many middle-class black families. The man may have been present as *de facto* head, but this did not indicate that he was the leader of the family. The system of racial stratification was too pervasive to allow many black families to escape unscathed. For example, segregated housing lumped all blacks together just as the system ascribed the same role to all black people. Because of housing segregation, the gulf between the middle class and the lower class was not so great as is often assumed.

One may then imagine that there was a struggle by the middle class to free itself from the influence of the ghetto. But the conflict was not so simple. The battle was not so much between a group of middle-class blacks espousing white values and a larger group of lower-class blacks with "immoral" ghetto values as it was a personal conflict within individuals between both sets of values.

Middle-class blacks in Los Angeles had not formed a true aristocracy, as documented in Frazier's *Black Bourgeoisie* (1962). There were not enough "old families" in Watts to form such a group. Unlike Philadelphia, New York, Chicago, and

Washington, where there were large groups of blacks at the turn of the century (many of whom were descendants of free Negroes who had lived in these cities for generations), in Los Angeles there were only a few successful established black families. One exception was Biddy Mason, who had accumulated a fortune in real estate in central Los Angeles before the turn of the century. Descendants of Biddy Mason and the family of Paul Revere Williams, a wealthy architect, plus a few other scattered individuals, composed the only light-skinned aristocracy in Frazier's sense of the term. Their presence was hardly felt in Los Angeles at the time of the riot. However, a sizable group of black *parvenus* claimed a kind of aristocratic status. Except for their membership in certain clubs and organizations, their social habits were indistinguishable from those of other middle-class blacks. Most were only one or two generations out of poverty.

The world of both the middle- and lower-class people of Watts was impinged upon by the dominant white society. The structure and functioning of Watts was directly related to the existence of white Los Angeles. One can imagine the community of Watts as a circle intersected by dozens of arrows representing incursions by white institutions. Each of these affected the functioning of family, friendships, and other social institutions in the black community. The following brief examination of some of the ways in which Watts and greater Los Angeles interacted indicates that blacks of all classes could not escape the often crushing impact of the powerful white world.

EDUCATION

Anthropologists long have recognized the consequences of education in the making of a social being. The process of socialization begins in early childhood. The adult is, in large part, a product of his culture as a result of what he has learned in his youth. Consequently, education was one of the most important incursions of the white world into the black ghetto. Ostensibly, blacks were formally socialized in the same manner as whites. Watts children were taught the norms of white society in schools provided by the city. Mainly white (and some middle-class black) teachers used textbooks and curricula aimed at guiding children to conform to the standards of white, middle-class society. There was nothing insidious in this process. It is the method of education in all societies. The only difficulty arose from the fact that the standards taught were imported into Watts; they were not indigenous. The white world of school was not consistent with the black world of the Watts child. He lived in an environment that made it impossible for him to conform to the mores he was being taught in school. His black parents fell far short of the standards established in the classroom. Black women did not play the passive roles laid out for American mothers in textbooks. Black men were not like the achievement-oriented white men about whom the Watts child read. This caused a depreciation of his parents in the child's eyes. The child was taught that white values, standards, and norms were correct, but found no one in the ghetto achieving white standards. The result was a denigration of his parents, his associates, and himself.

Prior to the riot the Los Angeles schools made no attempt to teach the history of the American Negro to the students of Watts. The children were consequently left with the impression that only white men were capable of making history. Thus, even the lessons of history seemed to teach that blacks were inferior to whites.

ENTERTAINMENT AND INFORMATION

The processes of socialization and education in Watts outside the schools were complicated by the influence of the mass media. Television, radio, and newspapers, owned and controlled by the whites, brought an alien world into the homes of Watts. This ordered world of successful and forceful white politicians, businessmen, and astronauts further undercut the stature of the passive, failure-ridden black man in the eyes of his family. This was not the aim of the mass media any more than the same result was intended by the white school board. It happened because the institutionalized goals of society stressed a success ethic while the social structure blocked some members from achieving that goal. The ramifications of this contradiction were extensive for the self-esteem of the black man, his role in his family, and his role in his community. Every day the mass media reminded blacks of their inferiority. Black women saw the American standard of beauty—straight blond hair, thin lips, small rounded nose—and, having found themselves ugly compared to that standard, they lost their self-esteem as women and sought other, less sexually oriented roles. That the black-owned newspapers in Watts were supported in large part by advertisements for skin lighteners and hair straighteners testified to the extent of the influence of white standards in the community.

LAW (SOCIAL CONTROL)

In each society there is a shared mode of behavior that distinguishes or characterizes the group. This behavior is enforced by social sanctions—the approval or disapproval of the members of the particular society. Each group has its own sanctions based upon the traditions of the community. Stemming from the customs of the particular group, social sanctions provide for the smooth functioning of the society. To be an effective, cohesive force in a community, therefore, social sanctions must come from within the group, must reflect its needs and peculiar institutions.

Unfortunately, some laws in Los Angeles were written by whites that make the accepted customs of blacks illegal. For example, it is illegal to loiter on the streets of Los Angeles. This law was passed, presumably, to check pickpockets and other petty criminals. In Watts, where the home environment was not conducive to entertaining (because of the number of children, the lack of chairs, and, not least, the heat in summer), black men socialized on street corners—an innocent practice for which they were often jailed.

A more menacing law, from the point of view of the black man, was the prohibition against marital desertion. In Los Angeles, a man could not abandon his wife and family without paying a heavy price in child support, alimony, and fines. The law, based on white customs, protected children and jobless wives. In Watts, the benefits of the law were not so clear. Desertion had long been the poor black man's divorce. Unable to pay legal fees incurred in divorce proceedings, he left his wife in the hands of state welfare officers. The welfare payments she received were larger than any financial assistance he could provide. Moreover, in many desertions, the black woman was probably earning more than the man. Here we find a situation where a man could have been arrested for doing what was logically and socially expected of him by his peers.

As with education, the laws of the white world did not square with the customs of the black. But since whites were responsible for educating blacks, blacks were put in the ambivalent situation of accepting both white law, as morally right, and black custom, as practical necessity.

WELFARE

The system of employment in Los Angeles provided one of the key factors to an understanding of the social structure of Watts. We can see how the economic environment outside the community was partly responsible for the family and political structure within the community. This is true primarily because, on the average, black women were more easily employed than black men. Additionally, black women were also the recipients of the bulk of welfare funds, and welfare was one of the prime sources of income in Watts. The result of these factors was that the black woman very often played the role of breadwinner in the home. In Watts over 30 percent of the population received welfare. The system that until 1962 paid only deserted women added strain to the already tenuous marital bond. A system that was devised for whites, not for blacks, therefore, caused internal conflict within the black community. A Watts woman commented about another woman who was on welfare: "All those nigger girls know how to do is have babies." This attitude was fostered unconsciously by welfare officers (who were usually whites or middle-class blacks) whose only contact with the ghetto was in a paternal or policeman role, and who consequently seldom understood the fissures in Watts families and in the community that were caused by welfare. The effect on the self-esteem of blacks who were on welfare was unquestionably great. Many people in Watts told of humiliating experiences with welfare officers who cross-examined them to see if they were "cheating" the system by working.

EMPLOYMENT

The exaggerated role of welfare in the community is best comprehended by examining employment statistics in Watts. At the time of the riots, unemployment in the area fluctuated between 12 and 18 percent (in contrast to 3½ percent for Los Angeles as a whole). The underemployment figure, which was made up of those employed part-time while looking for a full-time job, those receiving a substandard wage, and those on short-term employment, was as much as three times the unemployment rate. Employment accounted for the largest numbers of black excursions into the white world. The few black-owned businesses in Watts in the preriot period—barber and beauty shops, pool halls, and bars—provided less than 5 percent of the jobs held by blacks. White-owned factories in South-Central Los Angeles and white businesses outside the black quarter accounted for nearly 80 percent of Watts employment, while federal, state, and local governments provided about 17 percent. Nearly 42 percent of Watts men, including some who were unemployed, belonged to labor unions. This fact is important to our study when we realize that almost all of these unions were national or regional organizations run by whites.

HEALTH

The picture we are developing, one of blacks almost totally dependent on whites, is brought into sharper focus when we find that there was no hospital for the population of 260,000 in South-Central Los Angeles at the time of the study. The closest hospital was thirteen miles away, or an hour from Watts by bus. The few black doctors and dentists in the area were largely shunned by blacks in favor of white doctors, who they believed were more competent. Thus, most people traveled outside Watts for medical care. The ghetto core had one fifth the number of doctors per capita as the rest of the county, yet this small number was dealing with, among other health problems, the highest rates of infant mortality, tuberculosis, and venereal disease in southern California.

SHOPPING

It is evident that Watts was an incomplete community in many ways. Although more distinct socially than almost any other community in greater Los Angeles, it was one of the least self-sufficient. Watts had only a very few markets and no large shopping centers, department stores, or cinemas. The few small shops were mainly owned by Jews, who did not live in the community. In a society in which mass buying and consolidation by major retailers brought cheap, fresh products to the white consumer, the shopper in Watts had to buy from overpriced specialty shops. The lack of shopping facilities was often given by residents as a reason for rioting and for their unhidden anti-Semitism.

In this chapter I have discussed the similarities in the roles of lower- and middle-class blacks. Both earned less than similarly ranked whites, lived in segregated neighborhoods, and were considered inferior to whites. In both classes black women were in more favorable economic positions than the men. Both classes of black women tended to have a more powerful status in their homes than women in white families. Because of this, black men, who were socialized to the belief that the husband should earn more than the wife and be "boss" of the house, suffered from denigrated self-esteem. In the eyes of whites, both classes of blacks were "niggers"—inferior, base creatures. Because both classes accepted white values, most blacks tended to look upon other blacks—and, by extension, themselves—as "niggers." At the root of this problem were the pervasive system of white values and segregation, the incursions of white institutions and values into the black world, the low market value placed on the services of black men, and the uprooting of institutional life caused by migration.

5 / Watts families

The statistics of black ghetto life in America are depressingly familiar: low incomes, poor education, high rates of disease, chronic unemployment. This human misery, and its effect on family life, has been well documented by many writers, both black and white. What is described in this chapter will be familiar to those who know something of the problems of blacks in poverty areas. Telling the story of the families of Watts is necessary if we are to understand the cultural nationalism that developed there after the riots. Important for the purposes of this study is the *déjà vu* quality of this chapter in light of the previous examination of Woodstock. One becomes easily confused. Is this South Africa or America?

Following are case studies of two black families in Los Angeles. The differences in life-styles between the lower-class Nelsons and the middle-class Houstons are obvious; more important are those aspects of family roles common to both households. The men in both families experienced continued difficulty in securing and holding employment, and in both families they suffered from depressed self-esteem and social impotence. The women in both families earned higher wages than the men and were instrumental in the struggle to provide a good life and education for their children. Both families were fighting against the ghetto morality and had internalized white values, the Houstons to a greater degree, perhaps. Finally, individuals in both families felt that other blacks were inferior.

These families are not typical of those sociologists usually use to illustrate black family life. The Nelsons were a stable family headed by a loyal and loving, if ineffectual, father. Such a family was chosen because statistics indicate that a male was present in the majority of Watts families in 1965, contrary to the commonly held belief that the norm for lower-class blacks was an absent father. The middle-class family, the Houstons, was not headed by a stern patriarch, the model made famous by Frazier (1962). Based on personal observation, it would seem that the norm for the middle-class black family in Los Angeles was for the male to have been present but to have played a more subordinate role than the male in the typical white family.

THE NELSONS

Joe Nelson, forty-two years old, is an inarticulate, friendly, brown-complex-ioned man who has no apparent interests in life. He was born in a small town in central Texas and held many odd jobs before he was drafted into the Navy during World War II. After the war he drifted between menial jobs until he was recalled into service for the Korean conflict. During his eight years in the Navy he received only one promotion. Currently, he is a part-time janitor in a local school. During his off hours he spends as much as eight hours a day watching television while languishing in bed. He seems absorbed in the old movies he watches, but when I questioned him about them, he was unable to explain obvious relationships between characters. His absorption probably indicates bemusement rather than actual interest in the programs. He is totally devoted to his wife and children and only occasionally stops to exchange banter with the men at nearby street corner hangouts. His wife says his place is with his family and insists that he come straight home after work, which he does, seemingly without reluctance.

His wife Mary, a year younger and slightly lighter in skin color than her husband, is from the same type of rural, southern background. (Mary and Joe are both in occasional contact with their mothers, who still live in the South.) She is the head of her household. She quite bluntly tells anyone who will listen that she is the one who keeps her family together. Daily she harangues her six children and husband on the subject of her enduring struggle to keep the children "off the streets." Mary constantly exhorts her children to beware of the dope pushers, gamblers, and other shady characters who people the streets of South-Central Los Angeles.

After Joe was discharged from the service, the Nelsons moved to Los Angeles. Because Joe was unable to find work, Mary had to seek employment before their meager savings were depleted and the family faced eviction and starvation. She heard from friends that a hospital for alcoholics needed a cook. She presented herself to the director of the hospital, who told her she must take an arithmetic test to see if she was capable of doing the calculations required in cooking for large numbers of people. In her words: "I told that man I couldn't do that test but I could do the cooking. I told him that through experience I could estimate how much food to use. I talked him into letting me prove it to him by cooking a meal. I got that job, I'll tell you. White people are degree crazy. Ain't no university ever gave a degree in common sense. I've got more common sense than most of those uppity folks with a string of degrees." Mary insists that her family recognize that she is the font of all wisdom for their little circle. When she barks an order at Joe he obligingly complies. She is as stern and authoritarian with her children as she is with her husband. She alternates this imperious attitude with warm, loving phases and what she calls her "sacrifices." Her current sacrifice is an animal farm for the children in the backyard. She feels that the responsibility involved in taking care of the animals will give the children a "sense of direction." The monetary sacrifice involved in supporting a cow, goats, chickens, and ducks is great, but she says she is willing to continue for the sake of her children's morality. Another sacrifice she made was the purchase of an expensive set of encyclopedias which she was certain would spark the imagination of her brood and send them down the road to academic achievement. A year after their purchase the books sit dusty and forlorn, partly covered by old newspapers and pulp magazines.

Mary Nelson hardly seems to be aware that her efforts to save her children from the culture of the street are not succeeding. Although the children obey her out of fear while in her presence, her moralizing has little effect on them outside the house. In school and on the street the Nelson children are indistinguishable in their behavior from other ghetto youths with less concerned mothers. Joe Jr., sixteen, the oldest boy, is as diffident and inarticulate as his father. He is nearly illiterate, although he has had the benefit of ten years in Los Angeles public schools. He takes barbiturates and other pills that circulate in the high school yard and was once suspended for a month for being drunk in class. He has been to juvenile court for petty theft and other mischievous behavior. He does not date girls, and there are signs that he may have been affected by his younger sister's blatant sexual behavior. Joe says he might like to become a farmer.

His sister Rose is a fifteen-year-old whose only communication with others is through sex. She walks around the house naked or in a near-naked state while her mother cries futilely at her to cover herself. Rose comes home late and, whenever her mother turns around, she disappears to meet her boy friends. When Rose did not come home for three days her mother cried for a few moments then shrugged her shoulders saying philosophically, "She'll come home when she's pregnant."

The Nelson twins, aged thirteen, have contrasting personalities. One is a slow, desultory youth who resembles his older brother and father. The other is an intelligent, hard-working boy who is the only one in the family successful in school. He does his homework without his mother's urging under trying circumstances of noise, poor light, and no table on which to work. Significantly, he is the only member of the family to show any outward signs of hatred of whites.

The eleven-year-old brother is quiet, obedient, and devoted to the backyard farm. The nine-year-old boy, Johnny, is the only child who is open, talkative, and lively in the family. His behavior in all ways is similar to that of a white child of his age. His mother says, "All the boys were like that when they were Johnny's age."

Although the Nelson family is tightly knit in the sense that the members spend most of their time together, there is very little verbal communication among them except for the completely one-sided tirades of Mary Nelson. Neither as a family unit nor as individuals do they appear to talk over their problems or share thoughts. All eight members of the family often sit in or on the bed watching television together, but except for Mary or little Johnny, no one talks. They do not dine *en famille;* they eat alone at irregular hours, each fending for himself.

At the time of the riots, the Nelsons were going through a transition period. Mary had secured a job with a government welfare agency. She was earning more than twice Joe's salary. By combining their salaries, they had been able to place a down payment on their wood-frame house and the half acre of land on which it stood. Their new affluence made them a target for theft in the community. Within a month after Mary Nelson received her first paycheck their house was robbed three times. Once, all the meat from a freshly slaughtered backyard pig was stolen from their freezer. The battery from Joe's old pickup truck that he uses on odd jobs was also stolen. None of the robberies was reported to the police. Mary explained, "The police don't care and, anyway, how are you going to find out who did it? Everybody down here steals. I just don't understand these Negroes. They have no morals. All they care about is having a good time. If parents set a better example for their kids, then we wouldn't have all this trouble."

THE HOUSTONS

The Houstons consider themselves black aristocrats. They are proud of their light skins and include the names of white ancestors when they recite their genealogy. They own houses in the heart of the ghetto which they rent to poor blacks. The Houstons themselves live on the fringe of the ghetto in a racially mixed neighborhood that is ineluctably becoming all black. They live in two large houses on adjoining lots. The Houstons are headed by three middle-aged sisters who share the economic responsibility for their extended family. With the sisters live their unemployed husbands, their children, and a variety of more distant relatives, mainly children of their cousins whom they left behind in the South. (The southern cousins send their children to live with the Houstons in order that they may benefit from the better schooling in Los Angeles.)

The Houstons came to Los Angeles from the South during World War II. The three sisters had degrees from all-Negro colleges that qualified them to teach school in the North. One husband had a law degree from an all-black institution, another was a small-businessman in the South, while the third claims to have been "retired" at the time he left the South. The lawyer was unable to pass the stringent California Bar examination and became involved in Democratic Party patronage politics, which was lucrative as long as his faction of the party was in office. When his candidate lost the mayoralty, he "retired" and joined his brother-in-law in *dolce far niente*. The third brother-in-law worked for many years in the post office and retired with a pension.

By pooling their salaries as teachers in the well-paying Los Angeles school system, the three sisters managed to acquire enough capital to buy numerous pieces of property in central Los Angeles. Through cooperation and a shrewd business sense, they put themselves into a position where they could compete favorably with most middle-class white families. By ruling their home with an iron hand and inculcating the virtues of thrift and hard work into the family, the Houstons became economically "white."

Since arriving in Los Angeles, the brothers-in-law have seen their influence in their families slowly wane as the hard-working sisters gradually usurped fiscal and disciplinary authority from the feckless males. In addition, the sisters gained influence in the black community through their work in the Urban League, the National Association for the Advancement of Colored People, and through black women's sororities. The husbands are seldom seen and never heard in black society. The men find themselves "retired" to a quiet life of television and reminiscing. Their children look not to them for advice, guidance, and love but to the sisters who control the purse strings.

The three sisters possess a drive to succeed that is unusual even in success-oriented American culture. They are relentless workers who take little time off for recreation or such feminine activities as gossiping and visiting beauty parlors. They do not have time for regular dining hours. They eat on the run. They work late into the night on their accounts and at planning their next economic move. Jointly they make all family decisions. The most interesting of these decisions, sociologically, was to make their only male heir a success in the white world. With only one son among the three women they decided to merge their resources to make him a successful man, not only among blacks but among whites.

Milton grew up, in a sense, with three mothers. He would ask not only his mother for permission to do something, but his aunts as well. He would kiss all three of his mothers good night, ask for money for sweets from all three, and receive punishment from all three when he displeased them. In Milton's eyes, his father was a weak, dependent creature—a kind of lodger in his mothers' home. From an early age Milton's mothers told him that he must be successful in the world. They told him that white people would throw obstacles in his path, call him names, despise him. The women told him that he must never give up, that he must laugh off the derision of the whites, that he must drive himself. He must never be like the common Negro. He must be respectable. He must be white.

With money, guidance, and affection flowing from three sources, Milton made his way confidently among whites in school. The sisters made certain that he was better dressed than his white classmates, had more and better playthings, and more pocket money. Later, they made certain that he spent long hours at his studies. That he was only mildly successful at his school work was not from want of trying. When it became evident that Milton would achieve the standards necessary to assure entrance to a university, the sisters decided that he should attend an expensive, private institution famous for its graduates' later success in business enterprises.

At the university Milton shunned the few black students and associated entirely with whites. But he found that his affluence did not change the color of his light brown skin in his white friends' eyes. They were friendly to him but always brought up racial issues, made him defend black causes, made him be the black he did not want to be.

He believed that acceptance by a white woman would be a bridge to the white world. He would call dozens of white girls until he found one who would meet him for lunch or for a soft drink. When he was refused by a girl he told me that he would say, "You are only saying no because I'm a Negro." He would call back again and again until the girl would either relent under his persistence or fight back, often within a racial framework. His first sexual experience occurred with a white girl, but he admitted that he found himself impotent.

As he grew older the chasm grew between the white world to which he aspired and the black world to which his color relegated him. He would go with his white friends to restaurants frequented almost entirely by whites and impetuously demand special service from white waiters in a haughty, arrogant tone. Then, suddenly, he would leave his white friends at the table to joke with black busboys.

When his grades were insufficient to gain admittance to law school, Milton was overwhelmed by the possibility of defeat. He swallowed his pride and wrote to a top law school that he was a "disadvantaged Negro" but he felt he could do well if "given a chance in the proper environment of law school." He was accepted.

Milton was caught in a racial limbo between the standards of white culture ingrained in him by his mothers and the social reality of his blackness and his personal shortcomings that he concluded were due to discrimination. His dilemma became clear to his white friends while they were being entertained in his home. His young cousin talked back to him when he asked her to do something. He suddenly shouted at her in Negro patois as he grabbed and shook her, "You quit that, hear? You don't want my friends to see what a black-ass nigger I really am."

The Nelsons and the Houstons represent very different types of families, yet their shared problem of being black in white America transcended their evident class dissimilarities. Neither Mary Nelson nor the Houston sisters wanted their children to have to play the inferior role of the "typical" black. They felt that their children deserved the advantages of white children. Both the middle-class Houstons and the lower-class Nelsons saw clearly that education and family encouragement were requisites for their children's success, but the uneducated Mary Nelson did not have the necessary understanding of white culture to socialize her children effectively as whites. Nor did she have the financial resources to secure a "white education" for them. Instead, she bought an encyclopedia that she hoped would bring "white knowledge" to her children. The more sophisticated Houston sisters understood that it took a proper home environment, hard work, and a modicum of push to succeed in the white world. But this class difference in the comprehension of social efficacy pales in importance beside the similarity of the failure of Milton Houston and Joe Nelson, Jr. to achieve white success despite the authentic efforts of their parents. Their failures were a matter of difference of degree, not of kind.

The family is the subsystem in which children are socialized to fill roles in most of the other major subsystems of a society. The family is therefore at the core of the status system of American society. The status placement that occurs in the family relates the child to the broader segments of society. Lee Rainwater (1965) has called the family the "crucible of identity." The child learns who he is and how he must behave through imitation and interaction with his family. In the families of Watts, children were taught their social roles as blacks. From their parents they learned not to be aggressive or hostile to whites, and to support such behavior they were taught techniques of self-deprecation. From their families, black children learned the role of "nigger" that they were to play throughout their lives.

The Watts child learned his social role by watching and imitating his parents, and by comparing their behavior to that of others. He learned from observation that blacks deferred to whites, that it was dangerous to "cross" a white man, that blacks were inferior in appearance and moral worth to whites. His father constantly belittled other blacks, saying such things as "You can't trust a Negro" or, "All niggers are good for is fighting among themselves." His mother used bleaching cream on her skin and applied hair-straightening products in a futile effort to look white. When the child compared the ideal white parent—there was no ideal black parent in the society—to his father and mother, he found them singularly wanting in looks, behavior, wealth, and morals. Acceptance of the white ideal led to frustration: he could never be white, yet to be black was to be inferior. His borrowed values and ideals led to a destruction of self-esteem.

The young black woman "knew" that men were supposed to be able to support their modest and feminine wives. She "knew" that straight hair and light skin were the hallmarks of beauty. The young black man "knew" that men did not desert their wives and children. He "knew" that through hard work and perseverance any American could become successful. But white values clashed with black reality and left the young person with a dilemma: he could not identify successfully with either a white or a black model. The acceptance of white values made it impossible for him to identify with blacks because he would have been identifying with an inferior person. He could not identify successfully with whites because no matter how hard he tried he could never become white. At this stage of development—a stage young Johnny Nelson had not yet reached—the child had either to compensate for his inferior position or withdraw from society. When he perceived that he could never escape his dilemma, when he came to realize that his social role was entirely negative; when he came to hate himself and other blacks for being black, he felt the full and often crushing force of his inferior social role. At such a time, lower-class youths, like the older Nelson children, characteristically withdrew from society or adopted other forms of antisocial or retreatist behavior. Apathy, crime, gambling, alcohol, or drugs were often associated with this kind of self-hatred among black ghetto men; indiscriminate sexual affairs were the likely symptoms of the same problem among lower-class women.

Faced with the same realization of inferiority, the middle-class black, like Milton Houston, would often "play white," adopt ritual behavior, accept a world of make-believe, and conform to white values as closely as possible. Ritualism, a standard form of middle-class adaptation, occurs when individuals, perhaps realistically, have given up their aspirations but continue in acceptable institutionalized behavior. This was common among middle-class blacks who were "sham" whites. These people went through the motions of middle-class people at work, but out of fear of failure avoided really taking the risks of trying to better their social or economic lot. The Houston brothers-in-law typified this type of behavior. Robert Merton (1968) has noted that such ritualism may lead to a defiant outbreak after a period of overcompliance. Milton Houston's behavior in restaurants and with his young cousin could be interpreted as such an outbreak.[1]

Some black middle-class families, such as the Houstons, had achieved white middle-class economic status. Superficially their behavior appeared to conform to white standards. Their ideal behavior was in compliance with the white norm. Consequently, they made a claim of superiority over other blacks. Their "aristocracy" was a pretense, however, because they had not achieved middle-class status in the eyes of white America, their reference group. No matter how wealthy these aristocrats were there were places they could not go, things they could not do, jobs they could not hold. From their comfortable viewpoint they tended to look down on poor blacks. They saw the crime, violence, and illegitimacy of the central ghetto and decided that their black brothers were, as the white man claimed, inferior creatures. These aristocrats, however, were held accountable by white society for the sins of the poor black. (Reputedly, there were cases where middle-class blacks who lived miles from the central ghetto were summarily fired from their jobs by white employers during the Watts riots.) No matter to what degree the middle-class black isolated himself from the ghetto, white America would not recognize the distance. The middle-class black who was fully socialized to the values of white America was often forced to particularize his failures. When he was fired or did not succeed in the white world, he was inclined to say, "I am personally inferior. It is not just that I am black. If I had any personal worth I could succeed."

This thought process was particularly painful for middle-class blacks who were

---

[1] Another example that supports Merton's contention occurred during the Watts riots. A black scientist, who lived a "white life" in an integrated neighborhood with mainly white friends and work associates, admitted to friends that during the riots he loaded bricks into his car and drove twenty miles to the scene of the riot, where he took off his coat and tie, rolled up his sleeves, and hurled the bricks at white firemen trying to put out a blaze.

taught as children that black was bad but that they were nevertheless good. When the isolation of childhood ended and the middle-class youth discovered that he too was bad, that he was black, that he was a "nigger," he was crushed every bit as forcefully as the lower-class youth, perhaps more so. Lower-class children in Watts were taught from birth that they were evil, black, inferior, inherently bad. This form of socialization, unlike the middle-class form, at least had the value of saving the child from a later traumatic confrontation with reality.

Everywhere the ghetto child looked he found proof of his inferiority. He did not have to experience white prejudice firsthand; his mother told him he was a "nigger." Thus, the family functioned to support the entire social system. Rainwater (1965) writes, "In short, whites by their greater power, create situations in which Negroes do the dirty work of caste victimization for them." Kardiner and Ovesey (1962) project the low self-esteem of blacks as almost a closed system in which the acceptance of white values causes a self-contained syndrome of black hatred of blacks:

> Low self-esteem = self-contempt → idealization of the white → frantic efforts to be white = unattainable → introjected white ideal → self-hatred → projected onto other Negroes = hatred of Negroes.

In summary, the family was the "crucible of identity" for both lower-class and middle-class blacks. Although the two classes adopted different compensatory behavior when they realized the hopelessness of their inferior role, both were nevertheless responding to the same stimulus of institutionalized inferiority. In both middle- and lower-class homes in Watts the mother was the dominant figure. Upon her fell both the instrumental and expressive familial roles. It was she who had the primary responsibility for socializing her children to an inferior role. The Watts mother fed, clothed, and gave love to her children. She also punished them and taught them to hate themselves.

FAMILY PROCESSES IN WATTS

It was not without significance that the most popular expletive in Watts was "mother fucker."[2] In the black ghetto the mother was the central figure. In the family, in politics, in verbal imagery, she alone stood powerful against the social hurricane of the ghetto—she was the calm at the eye.

In white America the father's profession determines the status of the family. In Watts, however, lower- and middle-class families derived status from the mother's as well as the father's occupation. In Watts the mother either shared the instrumental family role or was the sole possessor of it when the father was absent.

[2] In shortened form one says, "you mutha." Similarly, in Woodstock a frequently used insult is "your mother's vagina." It is perhaps significant that invectives referring to one's mother's genitals are seldom used by males in patrifocal white society in America and South Africa. Among these groups the imagery is phallic. But it would be dangerous for Freudians to leap to any universalistic conclusions concerning this point. In lower-class Arab populations, which are patrifocal with a vengeance, "mother fucker" is a common expression.

In Watts the mother was the black family. In a sense, she was black society, since everything in that society focused on her. Sociologists even came to talk of the unnatural superiority of black women in relation to black men. The key to this superiority was employment. Black women were in great demand, until recently, to perform important tasks in white society. The black woman had been accepted into the white family as a domestic servant. Since the black woman presented no economic, sexual, or ego threat to a white society dominated by aggressive males, she had been allowed entrée—albeit by the tradesman's entrance —while the black man was forced to keep his distance.

The black woman had more power in society at large than the black man because she had greater access to the white world. Black men could not secure jobs because they were unskilled and barred from most well-paying crafts. Black women took essentially unskilled jobs that were not closed by race. They were more familiar with white bureaucracy, police, and welfare institutions, which gave them a definite advantage in society over black men. It was not simple sexual favoritism that caused black mothers to encourage their daughters to stay in school while discouraging their sons. They knew that higher education often meant only greater frustration for young black men who could not secure a post equal to their educational training.

Some sociologists have said that black women purposely rejected their less educated dependent husbands and sought to establish a matrifocal family that was more functional than an elementary union with an unproductive mate. However, the mother-centered family was more functional only because there was one less mouth to feed. Except for this, all other aspects of the structural form were dysfunctional. In fact, few women in Watts would have attached any advantages to being without a husband. They may have viewed men as untrustworthy, evil, and lazy, but they also considered them indispensable. To the Watts woman, nothing had a higher value than love. A woman without a man was seldom so voluntarily. The matrifocal family was not the product of conscious choice; rather, it was an adaptation to an unwanted situation, as the following case of a deserted woman in Watts illustrates:

> Delilah is about forty years old. If she were properly dressed and could afford false teeth, she would be a beautiful woman. Before her husband deserted her and their eleven children she kept up her appearance to please him. Even when she worked while he was unemployed, she tried her best to bolster his ego by pampering him and making him feel that he was still the boss of the family. She put up with his occasional lapses with other women and waited patiently and faithfully during the few times he was in jail. She even forgave him when, while drunk, he hit her and knocked out her front teeth. Now, living on welfare, she is too busy taking care of her children and too poor to try to improve her haggard appearance. She sits disconsolately by the window nursing their youngest child, hoping her husband will come back to her. But she is not optimistic. "I want him back, I'm lonely. I'm a fool, I guess, but I'd forgive him. Anyway, he won't come back. I've got nothing for him now."

The Watts woman may have been better educated than her mate, more acceptable to white society, more easily employed, and the head of her household, but she was hardly a well-situated, all-powerful matriarch relative to white society.

She may have been the kingpin of Watts, but to white Los Angeles she was a maid or cleaning woman. Consequently, black women too suffered from low self-esteem *vis-à-vis* white society.

The black woman's role was established at birth by the standards of white society. She could not be the narcissistic white girl sitting on the pedestal that she longed to be. By national standards, she was neither beautiful nor feminine. Her concept of her sexual role became as warped as the black man's. He was denied masculinity; she was denied femininity. The consequences were disastrous for the black family and community. The black woman was forced into an instrumental role from which she unhappily ruled her community.

There were at least three common domestic group structures in Watts in 1965. In all but one the woman played an instrumental role, and in that one there was a high probability that she would at least share the instrumental role. A review of the structural types of Watts families will illustrate the source of the power of the mother in Watts. The following three-part classification is not rigid, since a domestic group could experience several forms during its life cycle.

THE NUCLEAR FAMILY

The nuclear family represented the most common family structure in Watts in 1966. As the table indicates, 40 percent of Watts women claimed to have been married.

MARITAL STATUS OF WATTS WOMEN (1966)

	Number	Percentage
Total women, 14 years and over	8,240	100.0
Single	2,140	26.0
Presently married	3,300	40.1
Separated	1,180	14.3
Widowed	950	11.5
Divorced	670	8.1

The nuclear family typically consisted of a legally married man and woman and any children from their union. A popular variation on this family type was the companionate or common-law family, which was, when stable, nearly identical in form to the legally sanctioned nuclear family. In many cases, the structure of the black nuclear family was similar to its white counterpart, except in those instances in which the black woman played the instrumental role.

Using employment as an incomplete but verifiable index of instrumentality, it can be shown that there was a greater reliance on women for the economic support of the family in Watts than in white communities. The percentage of employed women who lived in Watts was nearly twice the number for Los Angeles County as a whole. Furthermore, the percentage of black women who held middle-class-status jobs was about twice the percentage of black men with similar occupations. These conditions tended to increase the strength of the woman's claim to the instrumental role in the family. One need only consider the black woman's superior earning power in addition to the fact that she received the bulk of welfare funds in Watts to find the source of her authority in the nuclear family. Her strength was, of course, nowhere near as great in the nuclear family as it was in the broken family. But from this evidence and the case studies presented earlier, it is clear that nuclear families, as well as disorganized families, could be matrifocal in structure.

THE EXTENDED MATRIFOCAL FAMILY

The matrifocal family in its most extreme form is called extended. In these units men were typically absent or only sporadically present and were minimally involved in the support and raising of children. Often such a uterine family approached what anthropologists call a matriarchal form. In such instances the family was matrilocal. A mother, her daughter (or daughters), and all their children lived together in the mother's house. Because of the confusion or doubt involved in naming children after their missing fathers, such families were, in a way, matrilineal, since occasionally the grandmother's last name was given to all offspring. Succession and inheritance passed down the female line. In this unique situation it was the mother, not the father, who transmitted the culture of the community to the children. In most societies the tasks of culture transmission are shared by various kin, with the most important "secrets" of the society reserved to the men. In the extreme matrifocal family in Watts such functions as status placement, biological maintenance, socialization, and emotional maintenance fell mainly on women. Differentiation among family roles was slightly matripotestal, with the grandmother or oldest woman (she may have been only forty or fifty years old) having a position of authority. There also may have been a low degree of specification of familial role obligations and rights. For example, the care of infant children would be shared by all members of the family old enough to participate in the various tasks involved. However, the grandmother in these families would often care for her daughter's children during the day while the daughter worked to support the entire family. If the daughter happened to be pregnant, it was not unusual for the grandmother to work while the daughter stayed at home with the children (her own, her sisters', and perhaps even her mother's youngest children). In such families little shame was attached to illegitimacy. Mothers seldom rejected their pregnant unmarried daughters. A mother would castigate her daughter, perhaps call her a whore, and then treat her lovingly. It is quite possible that the mother had the same unfortunate experience. It should not be inferred that this attitude represented acceptance of illegitimacy—it was more one of resignation. The ideal even among such disorganized families was to marry.

THE ABBREVIATED MATRIFOCAL FAMILY

Deserted women appear in census figures under the headings for the single, separated, divorced, and widowed. The term "widowed" was a particular ghetto euphemism for "deserted." A woman who had been abandoned by or separated from her legal or consensual mate would either go to live with her mother or sisters or set up her own matrifocal family consisting of only herself and her children.

Elliot Liebow (1967) has documented the correlation between the black man's inability to assume leadership in a family and his low earning power. He tells of cases where men deserted when the family became too large for them to support. Similarly, in Watts, among poor blacks, family size grew steadily but no concurrent increase in the father's income could be expected. When the point of diminishing returns was reached, the values of the lower-class culture sanctioned a breakup of the family, possibly instigated by the woman. Middle-class black families, as we have seen, often stayed together for reasons of financial security without romance or even simple affection as a binding force. There was no such financial security associated with lower-class black unions, however. To some black women romance was an expensive luxury because it meant an extra mouth to feed. Therefore, when the romance went, so went the man. In lower-class Watts the basis of unions was love. Nowhere in the Western world, perhaps, was romantic love more closely allied to cohabitation than among poor black Americans. Unlike the middle class, one seldom found a poor man in Watts living with a woman he had ceased to love. This was one of the most essential class differences in family structure among blacks in Los Angeles.

Because the presence of the male was ephemeral, being based on something as fickle as the human heart, women learned to be self-sufficient. They learned never to depend on a man for anything that they themselves could do better. This limited the man's role in the family quite severely, for except for masculine affection and sex, the ghetto woman could provide everything a man could offer. Her admirable self-sufficiency, however, had some undesirable side effects on the socializing of her children. The missing or ineffectual father distorted her children's image of husband and wife roles. Black boys grew up without a strong masculine model. Such a lack can produce effeminacy, but in the ghetto it usually resulted in men who, like their fathers, were unable to have a lasting relationship with one woman. The black man was not socialized to fill a family role. He looked elsewhere, to the street corner society, for a role to play. Young girls, on the other hand, learned that they must play *all* the family roles. This tended to perpetuate an unsatisfactory system of female strength and male weakness.

Young Watts boys often expressed mixed feelings about their mothers. This ambivalence most likely stemmed from the fact that the mother tried to be both a stern father and a loving mother to her children. The mother conditioned and trained her son for the defeats and failures she was certain he would meet in life. She tried to destroy the success orientation the child learned from watching whites. Since it was the mother who taught the child in the matrifocal family, who prepared him to face society, it was she who taught him that he was inferior. Her own experience with men probably caused her to overdo the lesson. The result was that the mother-centered family was not a happy one for a son.

Neither did the mother-headed family provide a secure environment for young girls. The mother was usually so busy trying to do the work of two people that home life became unpredictable, unsettling, and disorganized. The children never knew when or if they would eat. They never knew which man would spend the night with the family, who their "daddy" would be, who would sleep with their mother. A houseful of half-brothers and half-sisters tended to confuse the child's sense of human relationships. Everyone became a stranger. The child was unsure of his various roles: He did not know his father; he was unsure of his sister; he was confused about his sex. It was not unusual for little girls growing up in these circumstances to have sexual intercourse before puberty. Their mothers could not provide a secure orientation in a chaotic world.

The perils of life in Watts were great for the unattached young girl living at home with her mother:

> Alma is a fifteen-year-old high school girl. She was raped when she was thirteen by her mother's boy friend. She lives with her mother, two brothers, and pregnant sixteen-year-old sister. Alma's mother says she thinks Alma is old enough to get a job and help support the family, "if she doesn't get knocked up like her sister."

There were not many "old maids" in Watts. Few poor young girls, in fact, were childless when they reached their majority. Although they often failed, most girls attempted to form stable, legal marriages with the father of their children. The morals of the society dictated that a woman must marry, and Watts women genuinely would have liked to have been married. But romance did not appear to be a strong enough force to hold lower-class marriages together permanently. Middle-class black marriages, with an economic footing, were far more stable.

THE MEN OF WATTS

In most societies, family roles are complementary, such as mother-father, father-son, husband-wife. In Watts, however, a son without a father was a normal occurrence. In 1965, 7,510 of the 15,320 children under eighteen were not living with both of their parents. Since an individual learns his family role from the reactions of another in a complementary role, it is evident that at least half of the children in Watts might have been expected to have some form of familial or sexual role confusion. Children in Watts often grew up with female models who were drab, defeated women fighting to earn a living. The men, whom the children knew more superficially, appeared irresponsible and fun-loving. The men of Watts have been described by an outsider as "the bright-feathered birds, the free spirits." This view could have been shared by the women of Watts who suffered from the philandering of the males. But the Watts man did not see himself as a proud, splendid peacock in full plumage.

For example, Adam was typical of thousands of black men in Los Angeles. He was not a "free spirit" flightily bouncing from woman to woman, but a broken, defeated man. He had found that no matter how hard he worked or what he did, he could not succeed:

> Adam is forty-five years old. He grew up in the South and worked there as a butcher from the time he was fourteen years old. He married a girl he had known for many years. Ten years ago he heard he could earn higher wages in

Los Angeles. He left his wife and children and told them he would send for them when he had made enough to pay their way west. When Adam arrived, he found difficulty in securing employment. He tried his hand at boxing in order to earn enough to send for his family. He was not a success; he found only enough butchering to pay for his own room and board. After a while he met a local woman, fathered a child but eventually left her for yet another woman. He now spends his nights alone in a bar. "Anyway, I've never had to take any welfare money," he told me. When I asked if he was proud of that accomplishment he retorted, "Proud? Proud's a white man's word."

The black man knew that he was a faceless cipher in his country. He therefore adopted behavior befitting his role. White society told the man in Watts that he was a nothing, a valueless creature. The black man, overpowered by the force of white society and taught to believe that everything whites say is true, through a process of self-fulfilling prophecy, became the invisible man that white society predicted. The process was economic, social, and familial. Each of these aspects of life, all the products of white society, reinforced each other, creating the conditions in which the inhabitants of Watts were forced to live.

The most important of these conditions was the economy. There was no separate and independent economic system in Watts. Blacks in Los Angeles had to rely on white business firms and industry for their employment. In 1960, only 2.3 percent of the employed men in Watts were in professional or technical occupations. There was a disproportionately high number of blacks in low-status occupations such as service workers, operatives, and household workers, while blacks were underrepresented in such higher-status occupations as managers, officials and proprietors, craftsmen and foremen, and sales workers. And it is evident that not only were the jobs that black men in Watts held of lower social status, they were also lower paying.

The urban lower class in Watts was characterized by complete economic defeat. Many men simply dropped out of the economy altogether and ceased to partake in what appeared to them to be a fruitless struggle, as the following case concerning a Watts man indicates:

> Cobbs is forty years old, an army veteran, and once a successful high school athlete. He worked as a carpenter for fifteen years, then suddenly walked out on his family and his job. He goes from woman to woman now, staying with each one as long as she will put up with him. He has not worked in five years except for putting in a day or two of labor for a few friends and on a cash basis. He describes his life now: "I move my clothes a lot."

White Americans tended to think of blacks in servant roles. So pervasive was the attitude that even some white northerners would call a black man "boy." Black women were seldom referred to as ladies. Even liberal sociologists, who should know better, persisted in calling black women "females." To the American ear, "Negro lady" was an oxymoron. A black man was seldom referred to as a gentleman or addressed as "sir." Black men, furthermore, often held feminine occupational roles in the white world, such as cooks, dishwashers, hospital orderlies, and other cleaning jobs. The black man, a potential threat to the white male, was kept in socially impotent, if not outright feminine, roles. Eldridge Cleaver (1968) has described the black man's role in America as that of a "black eunuch."

Servility and dependency were two traits admired by whites in blacks. Herein lies the origin of at least part of the Watts man's failure to be a successful husband and father: Men in society must play many roles. This plural participation is smooth if these roles are not contradictory. But the black man was in the repugnant position of having to be a "boy" in white society and a "man" in his home.

Few blacks coped successfully with this duality and the several other contradictions in their roles in white America. For example, the American myth exhorts a man to be aggressive, but an aggressive black man was defined as a "bad nigger." The American myth urges all men to be economically successful, but obstacles were placed in the path of the black by denying him an education—the *sine qua non* of future occupational success.

Nevertheless, the black man interpreted his failure in the way white Americans interpreted it—as moral laxity and inferiority. The black man stood damned by white standards that the social system prevented him from achieving.

The black was thus confused. He was free, wasn't he? Then why wasn't he equal? Given the gap between liberty and equality, many blacks and most whites concluded that it was personal inadequacy that prevented blacks from closing the gap. Theo Jones of Watts blamed black men for their failures:

Mr. and Mrs. Theo Jones, both nearing fifty, own half an acre of land in Watts. It is half an acre of dirt, actually, as no bank will lend Theo Jones a penny to improve it. Their house is a large, two-storied, wooden-frame structure, built in the Los Angeles Victorian style. It once stood imposingly in Hollywood, fifteen miles away. When it was too old to attract white inhabitants, the owners jacked up the entire house, put it on wheels, and rolled it to Watts. The house was fifty years old when it left Hollywood; it has been in Watts for ten years and has been Theo Jones's for five. Theo is proud of the old place, the biggest house in the neighborhood. Jones is a proud man, or at least he tells strangers he is proud. He tells them he is a plasterer who can make $300 working only three days a week. "I'm a skilled man. I'm not like these lazy niggers you see around here. I can work whenever I want," he says. In private, Theo's wife says that he actually had been unemployed for a long time before the War on Poverty began in Watts. Then the government was looking for buildings to use for the poverty program and spotted Theo's incongruously large edifice. Eventually Theo's wife was enlisted at a low salary to operate a Teen-Post (a place for black teenagers to gather under supervision). Theo's prejudices are now the rules of the post. He does not like teen-agers who smoke, drink, hold hands, or swear. "We only want good, clean-cut kids around here," he says, "just hard workers, no lazy niggers." As there are few ghetto youth who meet Theo Jones's high standards, the Teen-Post is a very large, empty place. Theo wonders why all the "good kids" do not come around to the post. Theo's notion of a "good kid" is his daughter, a shy, withdrawn sixteen-year-old who seldom leaves the house and has no friends among her age mates. Her sole interest is a large white dog. Theo does not mention his two oldest sons except to say "those worthless black bastards." They have been to jail frequently and one is a part-time narcotics pusher. "All these Watts people do is screw and steal from each other," Theo says. "Haven't they got any drive, any determination, any pride? Maybe the poverty program will get them jobs, that's what they need." Theo's wife, after patiently listening to him run on, interrupts him, "Well, they'd better find you a job first. You're the laziest nigger on the block. You're too proud to work."

In the 1966 special census of black Los Angeles, the figures for marital status in Watts showed an interesting discrepancy. Figures were reported for only 5,860 men, and for 8,240 women. Therefore, around 2,380 men over fourteen years of age did not report their marital status. Who were these missing men? Where were they? They were the street corner men, hustlers, and casual laborers who drifted from woman to woman. When they could not find a woman to support them, they lived with relatives or friends or, if they had money, as lodgers in boarding houses. They were the "free spirits" of Watts. But these men were hardly happy-go-lucky characters wheeling around in pink Cadillacs, as they were often portrayed. They were derelicts. They were made so because they were socially inferior and economically impotent. Because of this the black man of Watts could not perform his other masculine roles. He was not a man among men. He could not support his family. He lacked the confidence and skills to organize and petition to redress his grievances. In a society that measures happiness by material wealth, he could not offer a woman enough to eat, clothes to wear, or a decent place to live. In Watts he could offer a woman an overcrowded, dilapidated home, if he was fortunate enough to be able to afford even one of these. For the pleasure and privilege of living in a home with almost twice the number of people per room as a white home, the black man would pay almost the same rent as a white man paid for a cleaner, newer, and larger home. When faced with these facts of life, many black men took to the streets. They knew they would be failures in a home. They dropped out of normal American family, economic, and social life. To these men, alcohol and narcotics became a refuge from overpowering social conditions. To them, violence and casual sex became the proofs of manhood.

Violence and casual sex were day-to-day occurrences in the lives of poor Watts men, although not to the extent that was true in Woodstock. Sexual assaults and assaults connected with robberies and feuds were, nonetheless, commonplace in the experience of poor blacks. Richard, an articulate thirty-five-year-old street corner man in Watts, claimed that blacks were fools because they committed crimes against each other:

> I've been rolled three or four times. I always say to myself, why aren't these crazy bloods working over some white man? You can't believe the violence down here. Yesterday I saw a girl shot on the street by her boy friend. A pretty young girl, dead before we could call an ambulance. That's the worst thing about being black. White society has lowered the value we place on ourselves. Some people here wouldn't think twice about shooting a black man but would be terrified even to talk back to a white man. I've had every hustle you can imagine—numbers, dope, heisting refrigerators, you name it—but I've never hurt anybody physically. There aren't many guys down here can say that.

When asked why he did not marry and settle down, Richard laughed and said, "Marriage is a white institution. You whites try to turn Africans into white men. We're polygamous. It's unnatural for a black man to have only one woman." Certainly, Richard had his tongue in cheek when he made that claim, but he was not being altogether facetious. Monogamous marriage is not natural for a man who cannot benefit from the arrangement. All marriage did was drive home to the poor black how inferior he really was. "You can support yourself with a hustle," Richard said, "but you can't feed six kids and a nagging bitch."

Among street corner men in Watts the ability to "hustle" was an admired trait, indeed, essential to survival. Some blacks earned a living by shooting dice, others by conning unsuspecting whites and blacks with card tricks, and still others by selling narcotics. Another form of "hustle" was the ability to talk to women. Street corner men bragged about their ability to get a free meal, sex and even cash from women. According to the myth of ghetto masculinity, the mellifluous man could turn parsimonious, frigid women into generous, sex-craving lovers. But in reality it was probably loneliness that caused Watts women to take steps they knew they would later regret. The myth portrayed the man fed, satiated, his pocket full of cash, chasing off after another woman while the poor abused lover pined away for want of him. There was probably an element of truth in the myth, but it was not the literal truth as some have suggested. Black men were not nearly as heartless and calculating, nor as successful with women, as they claimed or as white observers made out. Cavalier behavior may have been reputedly admired, and the man who exploited women for sexual and material favors may seemingly have been held in high esteem by his mates, but his verbal bombast and sexual posturing were unsatisfactory substitutes for the kind of behavior the black man would have chosen if he could.

The image of the black man as the gaily adorned free-spirited peacock is an inadequate description of an individual doomed to failure in the economy, the society, and the family. We might go to Durkheim for a reconciliation of this contradictory image. Durkheim (1952) shows that egoism and anomie can be two sides of the same coin: "It is indeed almost inevitable that the egoist should have some tendency to non-regulation; for, since he is detached from society, it has not sufficient hold upon him to regulate him." Such detachment, which is sometimes called alienation, occurs when social norms regulating behavior are no longer effective, when people feel forced to adopt socially unapproved behavior. Anomie, or normlessness, results when the rules one has been taught to respect no longer serve as guidelines.

An anomic state will exist when institutionalized means to culture goals are blocked. The Watts man was socialized to want monetary success and play a masculine role in society and his family. But no matter how hard he tried, he was powerless to achieve those goals. A system fails to motivate individuals when it presents them with situations in which there are no clear possibilities of achieving defined goals. If an individual constantly finds himself in social positions where there is no possibility of action, he may well resort to deviant behavior or withdraw from any situation that contains the likelihood of failure.

SUMMARY

The Watts family failed in its function of preparing youth to cope with other institutions of society. The family is the most important institution in the shaping of the future behavior of an individual. It structures, coordinates, and integrates his behavior; it molds his personality. When the family breaks down, as it did in Watts, the young people raised in the community do not have the basic human skills to order their environment. A broken family does not cause crime, school dropouts, illegitimacy, and drug addiction. Each aspect feeds on and influences the other. But stable families are strong enough institutions that they can counter other, weaker forces of disorganization. In Watts, the poor family was often an impotent institution made powerless to give structure to the community because of economic forces that were the result of racial discrimination.

Because the value placed on the black man in society was low, he was unable to play an instrumental role in his family. Without a place in either the greater society or his own home, the man in Watts lacked the sense of self-worth that could have motivated him toward involvement in community affairs in the hopes that he could work to effect a change in his position in society. Instead, black men sat by fearfully, hopelessly, while black women tried to lead their families and the community. It was, as the expression goes, a vicious circle. When he was faced with this dilemma, the black man could only throw up his hands in explanation, as a young man in Watts did, and say, "What can you expect? I'm a nigger."

The next part of this study will examine the interrelations between low self-image, the dominance of women, family disorganization, and racial discrimination, as discussed in this part, and the political powerlessness of the people of Watts and Woodstock.

PART TWO | Politics

6 / Preriot politics in Watts

To the sociologist, one of the most striking aspects of life in preriot Watts was the relative lack of political organization. Since most important changes in a modern society or community come about through political processes, it is evident that social change in Watts was severely limited by the absence of the primary instrument of change—politics. In fact, prior to the riots of 1965, one could say that the citizens of Watts were powerless to effect most changes within their own community. The four hundred thousand black citizens of Los Angeles were, due to the unique factors discussed in this chapter, nonparticipants in the political structure of which they were an integral, if passive, part.

Watts, as noted before, was only a partial community. The institutions of the greater white community of Los Angeles permeated the black community, influencing the values, economy, and politics of Watts. In such social services as police, welfare, and schools, the white community had complete control within all-black neighborhoods. Therefore, to speak of preriot Watts as a community, it is necessary to redefine that term. In the accepted sense, a community has geographical and psychological boundaries. It is a spatial social unit with a congeries of social institutions. There is a tendency for the people involved to act together, or at least to act in similar ways. There are often strong kinship ties and organic interdependencies within the community and a degree of independence from the outside world.

Watts was not a functional community in this traditional sociological sense. William F. Whyte, Elliot Liebow, Ulf Hannerz, and others have shown that such informal social networks as peer groups operate in slum areas in lieu of traditional institutions. In the case of Watts, however, friendship networks were not nearly as well formed or prevalent as Whyte (1943) found in Boston and Liebow (1967) and Hannerz (1969) found in Washington. Although everyone in Watts had friends, it was difficult to see how these friendships performed the socially integrative functions that sociologists have claimed they fulfill in other ghettos. In Watts, friendships were too ephemeral and diffuse to give structure to the community. Unlike other urban ghettos, in preriot Watts there was really very little structural unity beyond the recognition that everyone in the area had one thing in common—his blackness. Later, I attempt to show how this concept grew into a base for political action after the riots.

79

The dearth of social and political ties within the Watts community before the riots is not an inexplicable phenomenon. It can be understood as an adjunct to the social problems already considered. The social forces responsible for the breakdown of the family in Watts were also responsible for the political disorganization of the community. The economic powerlessness of the black man to support his family was akin to his powerlessness to organize his community. Whites simply had a monopoly on the economic and educational requisites for power. And blacks believed that they were incapable of wresting any power from whites without these requisites.

The central dilemma of Watts politics before the riot, then, was that without power to start, blacks felt that no power could be generated. To the people of Watts, power was like matter and energy—it could not be created. Watts people perceived that power was in limited supply and that nearly all of its resources were held by whites. Without jobs and education, black men appeared powerless to exert their masculinity in their families or communities. Without education, which they believed would give them organizational skills, and money, blacks felt powerless to form a viable political movement. The lack of self-respect among the people of Watts was a by-product of this perceived powerlessness to influence the forces that directly affected their lives.

Pointing to the fact that blacks had little political and economic power, both requisites for manhood (success) in the United States, a young black man in Watts dramatized the situation by saying, "Really, I have no right to be alive." This young man's self-hatred was as much a problem of identity as it was a lack of power. With such an overpowering sense of defeat, it was unlikely that he, or others like him, could create any kind of a power base.

Sociologists used to characterize urban blacks as "aimless" and "apathetic." These attitudes were in part due to their dependence on whites, who they believed controlled every aspect of their lives. The politics of Los Angeles at least partially justified the blacks' suspicions.

The political structure of Los Angeles County is a patchwork of seventy-six different incorporated cities, ninety-five school districts, fifty police forces, and several hundred special districts, each fighting for a degree of jurisdictional sovereignty. Prior to the riots blacks were unable to establish themselves in this tangled system. For example, in 1959, not one incorporated town or one government department in Los Angeles County was headed by a black.

The city of Los Angeles itself is governed by a mayor, whose powers are circumscribed by charter, and a fifteen-man city council. City councilmen are elected from large districts that are reapportioned every four years. Prior to 1963, no blacks sat on the city council. In 1959, the only black holding elective office from Los Angeles was a member of the California State Assembly. No blacks representing Los Angeles were in the California state senate or in Congress. No blacks were on the county board of supervisors. Blacks were kept out of office, in part, through the gerrymandering of districts and also through the control of party campaign funds. A political fact of life in Los Angeles was that no major party would support black candidates (with one exception) prior to 1960, and, therefore, blacks seldom served in office. Even running from predominantly black districts, black candidates would find themselves easily defeated by whites, who had the organizational skills and the money to carry out a successful campaign.

But the failure of black politics in Los Angeles was not due solely to the machinations and power plays of white politicians. The people of Watts were not effective politically because, as a group, they had not undergone the type of political socialization enjoyed by most whites. Because of their low socioeconomic position in the community, blacks did not learn how to participate in the democratic society around them. As with many poor groups, the people of Watts did not believe that the political system could effectively change their lives. They did not learn the skills of organization that middle-class whites received almost as a right along with the franchise. Poor blacks never learned that one can fight City Hall if he has the skills. Because their lives were mired in failure, they had little faith in their own political efficacy, partly because they did not believe that they, as a permanent minority in Los Angeles, had the power to influence the permanent majority. In a sense, because majorities get their way in the American system, the people of Watts saw democracy itself as working against them.

In some ways, the blacks' problem was not unique. Sociologists have shown that low-status persons are less apt to vote and less apt to belong to voluntary associations than high-status persons. Here the problem is more one of class than race. In Warner's "Yankee City" series (1941), the researchers discovered that the percentages of each class belonging to churches and voluntary organizations decreases with descending class status. Warner argues that all institutions of American society—schools, family, churches—are organized largely to teach people to "get ahead." Since participation in Watts in all these institutions was less than the equivalent white community participation, the political socialization of the blacks and, hence, their upward mobility, was severely limited. Blacks simply did not belong to the institutions where they could learn the arts of political efficacy.

The situation was further hampered by the matriarchal structure of Watts. It would have been surprising in an American context to find men effectively leading their community when they were unable even to lead their own families. For this reason, black women were the only power brokers in Watts. Black men had learned to relate to power figures—white men and black women—but they had not learned how to lead themselves. The voices of black men were not heard in their homes because they could not fulfill the instrumental family role. Their voices were not heard in their community because they had no power base. The problem of leadership was, therefore, one of the most pressing problems facing black men in preriot Watts.

A common lament in Watts was the lack of effective leadership. "We've got leaders, all right," a black social worker said, "it's just that they're self-appointed leaders, or appointed by whites. There are no authentic leaders chosen by the people." The primary problem of leadership in Watts was that of authenticity. Low-status blacks would not accept as genuine a middle-class black who they suspected was successful because he was acting as a "front" for some hidden white man. They wondered aloud what the successful black man must have done for whites to have "allowed" him to emerge in a leadership position. The people of Watts referred to influential blacks as being "owned" by white men. The suspicion was founded on fact—certainly whites were not going to encourage those blacks whose beliefs were inimical to their self-interest—and on political naiveté—politics is, after all, based on compromise. In Los Angeles, all black politicians owed their positions to whites who held the power in the greater community. In the eyes of the community, these black "leaders" were politicians first and blacks second. Some of these men were so flattered to be recognized by whites as leaders that they failed to represent black aspirations out of fear of jeopardizing their positions. The depressed people of Watts wanted their leaders to be blacks first and not politicians first. The reciprocity of the political system appeared to the unemployed, hungry, impatient people of Watts to be a "selling out." The truth is that black politicians had to be loyal to all the people responsible for their election and, therefore, could not fight so strongly for black causes that they ignored party discipline. But blacks who were accustomed to being literally sold down the river by their black brothers were suspicious of any black man who dealt with whites. This problem, too, may be related to class status. Herbert Gans (1962) has noted that lower-class Italians in Boston were also suspicious of their own leaders who become too intimate with the Yankee power elite.

But it was true, as the people of Watts were all too aware, that no black political organization was going to survive without some white support. In preriot Watts it is doubtful that one organization that was not primarily social or religious ever survived for more than a year or two without substantial white support. In fact, a requirement for a successful organization was recognition of the group by whites. Concomitantly, a black was a leader only if whites said he was.

Both blacks and whites in Los Angeles expected dynamic black leaders to emerge and lead the blacks from the wilderness. Whites, in anticipation of this event, often credited "Negro leaders" with more power than they really had in their communities. The result was frustration for the so-called "Negro leader." He was damned by the mistaken whites because he could not "produce results" in black areas and damned by blacks for being the tool of the whites. All potential black leaders found themselves headed onto the horns of this dilemma because, to be effective, they had to turn to whites for money and prestige. To do something effective for their own community, black leaders had to persuade whites to take action. Since there was no apparent power to act within the black area, the black leader had to petition whites as the representative of his community. He had to go with his hat in his hand if he was to succeed. But if his constituents saw their "leader" with his hat in his hand, he lost their respect. This was the state of politics in Watts before the riots. The political disorganization of the community was almost entirely a product of black dependence on whites.

The Watts leader's position in his own community was further weakened by the acceptance by his constituents of white stereotypes and prejudices concerning black people. A problem inherent in black politics was the acceptance by blacks of the white tenet that all black men were equally base. Blacks, who had been conditioned to accept this statement, had come to believe in the equality of all black men. Leadership, then, became impossible. A black man would not easily accept an inferior position to another black man. Black culture stressed that all black men were brothers. Such a philosophy worked against establishing hierarchical structures in the community. Only whites, therefore, could command respect. As Shibutani and Kwan (1965) have noted, throughout American history one sees "the disintegration of underprivileged minorities into bickering factions as soon as the more ambitious become able to better their lot." This process was particularly marked in Watts, where the rank and file were generally of the lowest economic class in American society while the black leadership group was predominantly middle class. Since the needs of the two classes were not identical, the poor people of Watts tended to feel that their leaders were working for status ends, such as integrating white neighborhoods for middle-class blacks, instead of welfare ends for their constituents, such as building better low-cost housing in all-black neighborhoods. There were also divisions within the middle-class black community stemming from the limited number of power positions available in the ghetto. One had to be exceptionally strong, even ruthless, to attain and hold one of them.

In summary, the political system in general worked against blacks with leadership aspirations. Occasionally, whites simply twisted the law to make it impossible for blacks to run for office. Almost always the whites were able to control potential black candidates through their control of campaign funds. Most important, blacks received incomplete political socialization and thus were unable to form viable political organizations. In those few instances where a black emerged in what was potentially a leadership position, he was viewed with suspicion by lower-class blacks. These phenomena were linked with this central problem: without a tradition of effective political organization, the people of Watts were unable to build one. This is not to say that attempts had not been made, but rather that they had all failed.

Three groups were influential in the attempt to build a black political base in Watts: the ministers, the matriarchs, and the middle class. Their efforts must be understood to appreciate what has happened in Watts since the riots.

THE MINISTERS

The most successful all-black organizations in Watts were churches. This was true in black ghettos throughout America. Traditionally, churches were the only black institutions granted a degree of autonomy from white domination. Franklin Frazier (1962) has written that "the most important institution which the Negro has built in the United States is the Negro church." In and around the Watts area there were more than 150 churches at the time of the riot. The vast majority of these were "store-front" or "separatist" sects headed by poorly educated, self-ordained preachers. Their popularity seems to have stemmed from the opportunity they gave for self-assertion, self-expression, and leadership to lower-class blacks. Sometimes the store-front minister was a huckster who went into the church business because all other businesses were closed to enterprising but uneducated blacks. In almost all cases, these churches were not based on any definite doctrines but promised otherworldly rewards to poor parishioners who were quite aware that they could not expect their just deserts in this life.

The general political effect of these churches was to support the *status quo*.

When the minister inveighed against sinning, he referred to sins against society, that is, the rules of white society. The ministers taught acceptance of life's miseries and the existing social order. These churches generated a feeling of group identification among suffering blacks—as is epitomized in gospel singing, a central feature of the services—but the churches discouraged any kind of protest. In effect, these churches were nonpolitical in their orientation but provided a functional substitute for some components of political life, for example, leadership and group integration.

The larger and more legitimate churches in Watts such as the Baptist Church and the African Methodist Episcopal Church were far more political in their orientation that the store-front churches. In preriot Los Angeles, when there was no political organization in the black community, ministers had considerable stature among blacks because whites accepted them—for want of anyone else— as the legitimate leaders of the community. Prior to the riot, several black ministers were accepted by whites and blacks alike as authentic spokesmen for the black community. It was these men with whom white politicians dealt when they wished to "sample the attitudes" of the black community or ask for support in elections. Unfortunately, as the riots were to prove, these established ministers had followings mainly among educated and middle-class blacks, who comprised far from a majority of the black community. During the high point of the civil rights movement, just prior to the riots, the ministers appeared to be in positions of power in the community. However, their inability to stop the riots proved to whites that their power base was shallow, and they quickly fell from their privileged position of dealing with whites as the representatives of the black community. The ministers fell in the eyes of their black constituents when it became evident that their job was to endorse white-chosen black candidates but not to nominate them.

Kenneth Clark (1965) has suggested that while churches are the most pervasive institutions in the ghetto, they are impotent because they do not hold power in the greater American society. In Watts the issue may have been even more basic than this. Ministers in Watts were not even as legitimate as white ministers because they were not ordained in powerful, recognized churches with white memberships. In effect, except for the African Methodist Episcopalians, with fifteen churches in Los Angeles, most black ministers were not members of recognized religious groups. Consequently, as the black community grew more sophisticated, the leadership position of the ministers in Watts fell precipitously.

THE MATRIARCHS

The ministers' closest ally in Watts was the matriarch. In an almost symbiotic relationship, the matriarchs of Watts supported the ministers financially and through their influence in the home. The ministers reciprocated by observing the greatest degree of deference for the matriarchs. Some Watts residents spoke of "the preacher-women power complex" that existed because most women's organizations in the ghetto were attached to some church. Through these organi-

Store-front church in Watts located in a former cinema.

zations black women tried to teach their people to clean up their houses, get religion, be moral, and "act white." In reality, their message was the same as that of the ministers. What was remarkable in Watts was that the matriarchs were more effective in putting over the gospel than were the ministers.

Because of their legitimate power base in the home and, because of their sexual exception from the rule that "all black men are equally base," the women of Watts were the most respected leaders in their community. There was a woman behind nearly every effective organization in Watts before the riots. When the minister received the word from the white Democratic Party chiefs he passed it on to the women, who would organize the campaign in the ghetto. The women had the organizational skills and the influence in the ghetto—not the preacher. The minister may have been a sham churchman in the eyes of the black men of Watts, but there was nothing false about the credentials of the mothers. In addition, neither whites nor blacks in America ever fully abandoned the stereotype of the Negro woman as "mammy." The "mammy" was always, at least in literature, the most powerful individual in the white man's house. Only she could tell the master when he was acting like a fool. Perhaps more basic than this social fact is that black women had greater economic independence than the men. In Los Angeles this economic strength was manifested in the relative political success of black women and women-led organizations as compared to black men and their organizations. It seems that black women were capable of building organizations and supporting them with funds collected within the black community while black men either relied on white funds—and, therefore, white control—or ended up with an unsuccessful organization. In the Watts area prior to the riots there were dozens of long-lived organizations led by women, but, except for purely social clubs, organizations led by men experienced short lives.

The success of black women in politics in Los Angeles began in the 1930s when Faye Allen sat on the board of education. This success has continued through to the present time. In the early 1960s, Vaino Hassan Spencer became a municipal court judge and, in 1966, Yvonne Braithwaite was elected to the California state assembly. The success of these and other elected officials is probably related to the fact that black women were accepted in white-collar positions in Los Angeles for nearly twenty years before black men could hold similar jobs.

However, the greatest influence of black women was not on city politics but on the internal structure of the Watts ghetto. It was also here that the interrelationship between family and political systems was most evident. It seems that the women of Watts controlled political institutions because young black men were deprived of a stable male political role model on which to pattern their lives. Consequently, young black men were not socialized to play leadership roles, either familial or political. As the women of Watts picked up the reins of leadership in the family by default, they gained political control of Watts simply by stepping into a power vacuum that men were not equipped to fill. This is not to say that women did a successful job. Obviously, too much unwanted responsibility rested on the shoulders of Watts women. They played too many roles to play them all well. However, what little self-improvement and quasi-political activity there was in Watts prior to the riots was often organized by women and invariably administered by them.

The success of a woman's organization in Watts often rested on the personal strength of the woman in charge. The most successful of these grass-roots organizations were not structurally democratic. The woman in charge most often was good-humored, kind, patient, and clever. But she had to be an autocrat if she was to succeed. Watts women leaders seldom asked anyone to help them—they told them. In contrast, male organizations in Watts were usually so concerned with democratic procedure that their effectiveness was stymied by nullifying minorities. Women's groups in Watts were more concerned with ends than with procedure. When young whites first went into the ghetto to work for civil rights groups and later for the War on Poverty, they were attracted by the democratic principles of some of the so-called Negro leaders in the community. They quickly found, however, that if they wanted to achieve anything in Watts they had to swallow their idealistic notions and cooperate with the dictatorial "mammies." Significantly, the highest-ranked black in the government War on Poverty program in Los Angeles was Opal Jones, a very strong-willed woman.

The women leaders of Watts engaged in self-help programs that by nature did not attract publicity to their leaders. A casual observer in Watts would have been led to believe that the ministers and a few white-ordained middle-class politicians were the most powerful political figures in Watts. The people of Watts, however, were aware that it was the women "who got things done." In South-Central Los Angeles, groups that were little known to whites, such as the Watts Women's Association, the Avalon-Carver Community Center, the Mothers of Watts Community Action Council, Mothers Anonymous, the Welfare Recipients Union, the

Welfare Rights Organization, the Central City Community Mental Health Center, the Neighborhood Organizations of Watts, the South Central Volunteer Bureau of Los Angeles, and the Will Frandel Ladies Club of Watts, were all grass-roots organizations led by women and were all well known to the people of the community. Prior to the riots, such organizations were the only indigenous, effective groups operating in the Watts area. Such women-led groups raised their own funds from within the community (and also used available government and white-donated money) to promote youth programs, health programs, credit unions, job placement bureaus, voter registration drives, political demonstrations, and neighborhood improvement projects.

The women who ran these projects were, in the main, uneducated lower-class individuals whose primary qualification was strength. Most were middle-aged, unkempt, plump, and unattractive. A great percentage were widows or divorcees who were not competing sexually with the younger black women in the community. These were not aggressive young career women; they were the mothers of the community and to the community.

THE MIDDLE CLASS

Strong male figures dominate the business history of the United States, and in the American system a man proves his mettle in the market place. In Watts, however, the black man was denied the opportunity to prove himself in this traditional manner.

The economic situation worked against the formation of a strong, black middle class composed of businessmen such as existed in white Los Angeles communities. A former president of the United States once said, "The business of America is business." Business is the traditional road to success in America but this avenue was almost completely closed to blacks. Business was not the business of Watts. Middle-class blacks in Los Angeles were mainly lawyers, doctors, civil servants, and teachers. In Watts there was no entrepreneurial heritage; the biggest and most successful businesses in Watts were owned by whites. A classified directory of black-owned businesses in South-Central Los Angeles showed the largest number of entries to be beauty shops and churches. The vast majority of black-owned businesses were one-man or family operations such as garages, cafes, repair shops, and bars. The social result of such a shaky economic foundation in the Watts community was a dearth of middle-class citizens. Since the middle class in America is the breeding ground for politicians, Watts found itself leaderless.

Most middle-class blacks in Los Angeles lived miles away from Watts—although still in the black ghetto. Many of these people owned businesses in Watts, but they were small "defensive" enterprises, that is, businesses that did not compete with white establishments, such as funeral parlors, pool halls, and bail bond offices with all-black clientele. Since such enterprises were insignificant economically, this middle class wielded little political power in white Los Angeles. And because this group was not a significant employer of black labor, it wielded little power even within the black community.

Yet, this middle class, separated by social distance from the majority of ghetto residents, still composed the official leadership group in Watts. The women of Watts were the actual indigenous leaders of the community. However, they were not the "recognized" leaders because they were not "politicians" in the white cultural sense. Within Watts there was little political role differentiation, that is, there were no full-time politicians. No one in Watts could afford to be a professional politician—there was no organization to pay him. The black middle class did, however, provide "politicians" for Watts with the aid of the Democratic Party. Thus, the authentic, local political structure of the community was bypassed in favor of a foreign element, the middle-class black politicians.

Middle-class blacks were more effective organizers than lower-class blacks. Significantly, however, middle-class black organizational skills were not as advanced as those of middle-class whites. The difference occurred because middle-class black institutions were, in David Riesman's terminology, "caricatures" of white institutions. In Los Angeles the most powerful and longest-lasting middle-class black groups were university fraternities and sororities modeled after white organizations. Alumni of white fraternities in Los Angeles tended to have only a sentimental tie to their former club and normally limited their activities to one homecoming visit a year and a small donation. Black fraternities and sororities were far more serious institutions. They were *run* in the ideal way the constitutions of white organizations only *read*. Middle-class blacks took old school ties, secret handshakes, and oaths of brotherhood until death as serious matters. Many literally lived for their club or lodge or fraternity. A good share of this attitude was a misreading of the way they thought white organizations were run. The end result was that these clubs were a parody of white institutions. Another result was that middle-class blacks developed a high degree of loyalty to and willingness to work for certain institutions. In Los Angeles, the Democratic Party benefited as much as anyone from the loyalty of middle-class blacks.

The Democratic Party in Los Angeles is an uneasy coalition of blacks, Mexican-Americans, Jews, lower-middle and middle-class white workingmen and union members, and upper-middle and upper-class white intellectuals. Nominally, these groups compose the majority of the electorate in the city. In reality, the only group that can be counted on to deliver 90 to 100 percent of its votes to the Party at election time is the blacks. Their loyalty is uncontested.

The close alliance between black Angelenos and the Democratic Party is not of long standing, however. The first successful Negro politician in Los Angeles, Augustus Hawkins, found it necessary to court Republicans as well as Democrats in his first campaign for a seat in the California state assembly in 1934. Hawkins has represented the black people of South-Central Los Angeles for over thirty-five years, first in the Assembly and, since 1962, in Congress. However, he is not a Watts man in any respect. He is very light-skinned, conservative in dress and manner, and middle class in background. He is a Negro only because he claims to be one. Hawkins has little contact with the poor people of Watts. He has never built a political machine in the ghetto nor has he developed a professional staff in the black area. Because he was the only black candidate with white support (that is, money), Hawkins was elected. Prior to 1960, the congressional districts of Los Angeles had been apportioned to prevent a black majority in any district. After the Democratic sweep in 1960, Hawkins was "rewarded" for Watts having voted 92 percent for Kennedy with a reapportionment that gave blacks a majority in one congressional district, and Hawkins was elected. The important fact sociologically is that many people in Watts feel Hawkins' lengthy career has gone on over the heads of his constituents. They claim that they have had little say in his political life. In many elections they were not even given the chance to vote against him because he ran unopposed.

During the years Hawkins was a state representative, a white politician from an area adjoining the Los Angeles ghetto built an influential political organization in the state. By 1960, Jesse Unruh, then Speaker of the state assembly, was in the position of power broker with the black bloc of voters in Los Angeles. Between 1960 and 1966 Unruh had handpicked and financed the campaigns of at least six successful black Democratic politicians in Los Angeles: Assemblymen Douglas Farrell, Bill Greene, and Leon Ralph; state Senator Mervyn Dymally; City Councilmen Gilbert Lindsay and Billy Mills. Unruh must be credited with enlarging the representation and influence of blacks in California. However, it must be noted that his candidates were not home-grown products but rather middle-class party loyalists packaged and delivered from outside the central ghetto area. Although Unruh and his black followers demonstrated their concern for the poor people of South-Central Los Angeles, they were unable to gain the personal loyalty of their constituents. They were elected and re-elected because they were the Democratic Party candidates, not because they had the personal approval of poor black voters. To gain this kind of support Unruh would have had to construct a true "machine" with patronage to dispense and a local ward organization visible to the community. Since the laws of California expressly forbid partisanship at the city government level and limit patronage at the state level, Unruh was unable to build a Chicago-style machine.

Political scientist James Q. Wilson (1960) has written that although big-city-machine politicians are guilty of many legal and moral transgressions, they nonetheless serve poor, uneducated minority groups more effectively than do the more honest but more aloof politicians. Wilson reasons that the machine is more sensitive to the needs of its constituents because it is closer to them and is more willing to fight for them because of its maintenance requirements. The machine, once in operation, becomes its own *raison d'être* and is quick to keep its own mechanism oiled by satisfying the needs of the voters. Unlike Los Angeles, which is characterized by *ad hoc* groups that come into being in election years and forget the voters in between, machine-run cities promote and sustain party discipline, encourage give-and-take, build community unity, and recruit new people into the political system.

The lack of a machine in Los Angeles limited the participation of black voters. Many Watts people—perhaps the majority—felt that they got nothing out of voting. They felt that elections were a one-way process, for although their congressman went to Washington or their councilman to City Hall, low incomes, poor housing, and poor public services still existed. Watts citizens voted for a candidate, yet never heard from him until next election time. No improvements were made in the ghetto, and nothing was changed in their lives, no matter who was in office. These people felt that at least with the matriarch-preacher complex one was personally familiar with one's leaders—even if they were not much more effective than the politicians. It is estimated that in 1967 only 59 percent of those eligible to vote in South-Central Los Angeles were registered. Even this low figure represented an increase of 9 percent since 1960. Certainly a major cause of this low level of registration was that many blacks changed residence every year and therefore could not meet the residency requirements for voting. However, evidence shows that apathy was a greater factor than change of residence. For example, in the November 1964 election there was a state proposition on the ballot that, in effect, would have legalized discrimination in the selling of private homes. For this one campaign, voter registration in Watts jumped 11½ percent. (Incomplete evidence shows that voter registration in Watts jumped to the highest level ever—approaching that of white neighborhoods—during the 1969 mayoral campaign, in which a black was a candidate.) Such evidence indicates that blacks will vote when they feel that the choice of candidates and the issues concern them.

White control of the ghetto was a central issue not only in party politics but in such nonpartisan, peculiarly black political activities as civil rights. The Urban League, the civil rights organization most respected by whites in Los Angeles, had little effect on the people in Watts before the riot. With headquarters over ten miles from Watts, the Urban League was a thoroughly middle-class-oriented organization. The executive director of the Los Angeles Urban League was recognized by most whites as a leader, if not *the* leader, of the black community. The white dominated board of directors made certain that the Urban League was the best-funded civil rights organization in the city. They gave money and support to the director of the League, who in turn made no "impossible" demands on them. Consequently, as the director's reputation grew in the white world, he became more estranged from the blacks, whom he was supposedly trying to help. When he retired in 1967 after twenty years with the Urban League as an "official" leader of black Los Angeles, the people of Watts found it difficult to point to any substantive concession he had received from the white power structure. Within the ghetto his retirement was hardly noticed, let alone celebrated. At the end of his career the whites who had established him had come to realize that his power was chimerical. The Watts riots proved to whites that his moderation had no influence in the ghetto. The riots proved to blacks that he had no influence among whites when it came to soliciting their aid to rebuild the ghetto.

The middle-class black leadership in Los Angeles failed even to unite among itself to coordinate its efforts. In the twenty years prior to the riots dozens of attempts to organize black leadership aborted or failed to survive infancy. In 1951 the Urban League attempted to unite with the Los Angeles branch of the National Association for the Advancement of Colored People in an alliance called the Association of Community Organizations. This united front lasted less than a year. In the early 1960s numerous groups and individuals came together to form the United Civil Rights Committee. Composed of churchmen, politicians, and leaders of civil rights organizations, the group was representative of all middle-class factions, but it was out of touch with the needs, frustrations, and aspirations of the poor ghetto residents. (The group did, however, successfully work to elect the Reverend James Jones to the Los Angeles Board of Education.) The organization did not survive the 1965 rioting, during which it became evident that it was not a representative group. Other recent alliances, such as the Temporary Alliance of Local Organizations, the Non-Violent Action Committee, the Negro Political Action Association of California, and the Conference of Negro Elective Officials, have all had histories of mistrust, acrimony, and backbiting ending in premature disbandings.

In general, it is accurate to say that prior to the riots there was no indigenous political activity *within* the ghetto except for the matriarch–preacher organizations. The few strong men who were ghetto residents often were ineligible for political office because they had police records. The rest of the men grumbled about "the system" but passively accepted the *status quo*. Some groups, such as the Black Muslims, were highly organized and led by strong men, but they were inward-looking and basically apolitical. Politics in Watts was something about which men talked, but in which they never participated. The primary topic of this conversation was always "the occupying power," the Los Angeles Police Department.

The Department was the only subject on which all the residents of Watts had an opinion. In the dozens of conversations about politics that I had with black people in Los Angeles, the police were always mentioned as a primary example of white injustice. "Police brutality" was a phrase often on the lips of ghetto residents. In my opinion this hatred was due to an interaction sequence in which mistrust of police led to mistrust of blacks, and so forth. However, the people of Watts saw only one side of the problem (as did the police) and they felt that they were unjustly abused by police officers. As the police were the most visible representatives of white domination, they became the symbol of all that was wrong in Watts. In 1968, there were 4,000 men on the force, but only about 220 of them were black. At the time of the riot, the Watts area was patrolled by about 200 white and five black police officers. Incidents such as one that occurred in April 1962 when police shot their way into a Muslim temple, killing one man and wounding six others, symbolized the polarization between the police and the community.

The people of Watts were not basically antilaw and antipolice. There was an awareness in Watts that the police were necessary. After all, blacks were robbed and rolled at a greater rate than whites. Watts people sided with the police if they were stopping a hoodlum or a known criminal. What they objected to was the attitude of most policemen—they felt that most were prejudiced. It was not simply a case of head beatings but a lack of sufficient respect. Most blacks claimed to have had a bad experience with the police and complained of the officers' condescending attitudes.

I discussed the police with a group of blacks in a bar and their comments were more animated than on any other subject. The owner of the bar said, "I never believed all this police brutality stuff until the other night when two of my best customers, law-abiding citizens, were picked up on a vag [vagrancy charge] while walking home." Another man added, "Every Negro I know has had some trouble with the police. Usually it's just a word, like 'hey, nigger,' but sometimes it's more." Other blacks in the bar told about being stopped by police while driving through white neighborhoods. "They wouldn't have stopped us if we were white," added one man. Another concurred: "If I walk out of the bar on the way to work and a cop stops me, even if I'm innocent, I worry that I'll be guilty before the cop is finished. They look for trouble." A bartender said, "Yes, it's these young cops. They're so damned scared of Negroes that they act tough to hide their insecurity. I was locking the bar up one night and I turned around and found two gun barrels at my head. Man, if I had dropped my keys, I would have been dead." The bar owner added,

> But I sympathize with the cops' problems. Young Negroes are born into such a miserable world that they won't listen to anybody. Older Negroes have a hell of a time with this generation. Don't get me wrong, it's what the white man deserves for sitting on his ass for two hundred years. If he had taught these kids how to read and given them an equal chance to get a job, then they wouldn't be a police problem.

All the customers in the bar agreed that young blacks were unmanageable. "The teachers should be able to knock them in line," said one man. Then the conversation quickly returned to the subject of the police. The bar owner's assistant said,

> I was arrested one night because my liquor license had expired, so I asked my brother to bring bail money down to the station. My brother asked the police where they were taking me. They answered, "To central headquarters." My brother said, "Where's that?" The cops got impatient and said, "You know damn well where it is." Since my brother didn't know where they meant, he followed the cop car. As we were driving along one cop looked into his rear view mirror and said, "Who's that nigger following us?" They pulled my brother over to the side of the road and beat the hell out of him. They got back into the car and said, "That was fun," and took me to get booked. The next night my brother waited until the cop who had beaten him was alone and nearly killed him. My brother's serving six years for assault now. You know, he didn't even have a record before that. What burns me is the whole thing could have been avoided. When I saw central headquarters, I realized that the cop meant the "Glasshouse." Man, every Negro knows what the "Glasshouse" is and where it is. Why didn't that cop just say he was taking me to the "Glasshouse?" If he hadn't insisted on calling it central headquarters, my brother, who sure knows what the "Glasshouse" is, would not have had to follow the car. If that cop had just tried to talk to my brother, he wouldn't have been beaten and he wouldn't be in jail.

The owner agreed, then added,

> But that doesn't make all cops bad. The last three times I was stopped while driving the cops have been courteous and have let me go with just a warning. You know what the real trouble here is? It's that we never see the cops 'till there's trouble. They don't walk beats. They cruise around in cars. When I was a boy in Louisiana, we all knew and respected the white cop who was a part of our neighborhood. He knew our names, knew who the honest people were, and who the troublemakers were. Nobody knows any Los Angeles cops.

The trouble with the police underscores the black man's struggle to gain respect as well as it illuminates the lack of a true community structure in the ghetto. To the people of Watts the first step toward a solution to their problems would have been to have black patrolmen walking beats under the aegis of a black community civilian review board. These and other proposals were aired at a meeting I attended sponsored by women and preachers to try to open communications between police and the black community. The meeting was held in a school auditorium. A panel composed of two preachers and two women "civic leaders" was chaired by a woman who, as far as I knew, held only a minor post in a community center. Still, she was held in respect by all the hundred or so people there. It seemed enough to the audience that her only credential for authority was her sex and her support by the preachers. Except for one police officer and myself the entire audience was black.

The white police officer did not speak, however. He stood in the back of the room while a black officer gave a short talk on the problems of law and order in the ghetto. The main thrust of his speech was that over 40 percent of the city's murder, rape, and aggravated assault cases occurred in the black areas of the city. Over half the audience was composed of middle class, and other "respectable" citizens, the rest were street corner people, the young, and a few black militants. After the speech the middle-class part of the audience gave the officer a warm ovation. The others were silent. The chairman then thanked the officer for a "wonderful and informative talk." She spoke for about five minutes about the need for the black community to support the police, who were, after all, on the side of all law-abiding citizens regardless of color. Then she invited comments from the audience, calling on three middle-class people. Each in succession sang the praises of the Police Department and damned the "ruffian" element in the black community who gave the "good Negroes," the majority, a bad name. Each of these individuals spoke for about ten minutes. The chairman ignored the raised hands of the black militants who wished to speak. Finally, she recognized one who recounted several cases of police brutality and insisted that the police officer must offer an explanation. The chairman ruled the question out of order and an insult to their "guest." She called on a young man, who rose to say that he thought the black police officer's first loyalty should be to his people because white officers' first loyalty was to their people. He said he could not see why black people should act any differently from whites. He said that a double standard existed: "If a white man beats a white man, the case will be pursued with due haste by the police. If a black man beats a white man, it will be pursued with *undue* haste. If a black man beats a black man, it may not be pursued at all."

The young and militant faction of the audience hollered, "Tell it to 'em straight, brother," and, "That's the way it is," and some even said, "Amen." The chairman pounded her gavel and said, "If these interruptions keep going on we will have to cancel the meeting. We don't want rabble-rousers trying to break up our meeting. That's not the democratic way to hold an open meeting." The audience was quiet. It seemed that although the young people knew they were not being given an equal chance to be heard, their respect for "democratic" authority was greater than their desire to speak. When they finally were given the floor again after another fifteen minutes of praise for the police, a young speaker was gaveled down for using "inappropriate language" and the meeting was adjourned with an apology to the guests for the "untypical behavior" of some of the members of the audience.

Another meeting I attended was at a church, in which a group of parishioners had decided to start an after-school tutorial program for their children. In essence, what had to be decided was how to delegate the responsibility among them for making certain that the children attended. All this meant, in effect, was that some adult had to call the roll and to telephone the parents of truant children. The group debated for nearly three hours over power—who was going to run this, who was going to do that, who was going to speak when, who was going to have what title, who was going to be on what committees, and so forth. The group fought over procedural matters, continually giving rather impressionistic interpretations from *Robert's Rules of Order*. The conflict was resolved when a woman stood up and assigned the duties and responsibilities entailed in carrying out the program.

These two meetings give us a clue to understanding the political culture of Watts. Basically, one can say that since blacks had never been permitted to make any important decisions affecting their lives, they were unfamiliar with democratic processes. With this disadvantage, they fell into bickering or anarchy unless a strong person dictated policy. (Or, as the police meeting demonstrated, some blacks believed that anarchy was a real probability and dictatorially sought to head it off even before it started.) It is not surprising, then, that women played the same dictatorial role in politics that they did in the home. In a community that was not politically differentiated, one could expect political power to be held by the same people who had economic and social power.

Another reason the people of Watts did not partake in their own government was the relative lack of secondary institutions in the ghetto. Black Americans had been characterized as "inveterate joiners" by some sociologists. This was true, at least in Los Angeles, only of the small middle class. Writers on social matters from the time of Aristotle have stressed the need of secondary institutions to stand between men and their governments. The French, particularly de Tocqueville and Durkheim, recognized the need for such political pluralism. They indicated that voluntary groups and associations are the means through which individuals in industrialized, urbanized societies influence their government. No one man can have enough power in a mass society to make himself heard. In such societies, power lies only in numbers. It was precisely the lack of effective secondary institutions that was the singular mark of Watts society. Except for religious organizations and the women's groups attached to them, there were few cultural or recreational clubs or special interest groups in Watts that could band together to demand political action. Most groups in American society are parapolitical. When needed, the American Medical Association or the American Rifle Association become powerful political lobbies. Blacks, on the other hand, were powerless because they were divided.

In summary, the political response of black Angelenos before the riots was to accept what the white man proposed because they felt powerless to influence the decision-making process. The political culture of Watts was marked by attitudes of alienation, hopelessness, and powerlessness. Most people in Watts so believed that they could not gain power in Los Angeles that they had all but abandoned attempts to gain it. However, in 1965, the blacks of Watts discovered a source of power that is now helping them to change their political culture and influence the decisions of those who govern them. This change is discussed in a later chapter, but first I examine the political culture of Woodstock in the light of what we now know about Watts.

7 / Coloured politics

Although the Coloured people compose 54 percent of the population of Cape Town, they are as powerless as the 15 percent black minority of Los Angeles. Powerless majorities are common in the history of the world—particularly in colonial situations—but the predicament of the Coloured people is unique. They were, until recently, enfranchised citizens of South Africa with nearly all the rights of white men, yet they never made themselves felt as a united political force. Their political history since emancipation is the gradual diminution of their franchise—a nibbling away by whites at the rights of Coloureds. From political equality at manumission to disfranchisement in 1968, Coloured politics has been a downhill struggle. By contrast, American blacks have been slowly but steadily winning greater political rights since the Civil War.

Politics in Woodstock today exists within the historical framework of Cape politics. Historically, whites have prevented Coloureds from forming their own political institutions by holding out the promise of integration. This outstretched hand caused Coloureds to become dependent on whites, who promised equality in exchange for loyalty. But all the Coloureds ever received from white politicians in exchange for unquestioned loyalty were broken promises. Yet, this did not spoil the faith of the Coloureds in the good intentions of the whites. It appears that the hope of being accepted as white was so important to the Coloureds that they could overlook any political setback as long as there was the chance of integration in the distant future. One comes to realize how much the Coloured people desire integration when one reads of the harsh laws and restrictions enacted against them and finds that they still have not hardened against the whites.

In 1833, the British emancipated the slaves in their colonial possessions, and two years later Coloureds voted freely in a Cape Town municipal election. Political equality was off to a good start in the old Cape Colony, but when a degree of self-government passed to the Cape in 1853, a moderately high property and economic qualification was added to the franchise. In 1887 and again in 1892, these qualifications were tightened. By 1909, the Coloureds made up only 11 percent of the electorate in the Cape, although they constituted 44 percent of the population.

In that year, the Coloured people made their first and last concerted effort to preserve their rights. When white South Africans announced they were prepared to pass a bill that would deny nonwhites the right to be members of Parliament, a delegation of Coloureds went to London to ask the British government to intervene on their behalf—on the grounds that Coloureds were loyal, civilized, British subjects. They received some encouragement from the British government, but when they returned to South Africa their hopes were destroyed. The South African Parliament passed the bill in the face of a British government reluctant to intervene in the politics of the newly formed Union. Nevertheless, a member of the delegation to London, Dr. A. Abdurahman, the founder of the only successful Coloured political organization, the African Political Organization, continued to fight for the rights of his people, but Coloureds were never again united as they were in 1909.

Abdurahman continued to serve as one of only two nonwhites ever to sit on the Cape Provincial Council, and he was the only nonwhite member of the Government Commission of 1937 that looked into the problems of the Coloured people. For all of Abdurahman's perseverance, he was never able to organize his own people into a united force, nor did he ever win any major concessions for his people from the government.

Abdurahman's efforts were vitiated first by the British and then by the Afrikaner promises of integration that undercut his attempts at organization. "Why push and ruin our chances?" was what the Coloured people felt, and the white political leaders of the Union did everything in their power to encourage such thinking.

In 1925, Prime Minister General J. B. M. Hertzog said:

> In this respect we have to remember that we have to do with a section of the community closely allied to the white population, and one that is fundamentally different from the Natives. He owes his origin to us and knows no other civilisation than that of the European (although he is sometimes lacking in appreciation of it), and even speaks the language of the European as his mother tongue. There can thus be no talk of segregation. That is the reason why, during the last seven years, the Nationalists in Parliament have held the view that Cape Coloured people must be treated on an equality with Europeans—economically, industrially and politically.
>
> The result of this policy has been that an alliance between them and the native population has been stopped. Luckily they felt that their interests were more closely allied to those of the European than that of the Native. It is their wish just as much as it is ours that they should stand by themselves with regard to the franchise.
>
> He is on the same footing in the Cape as the white man. This has not been the case in the other Provinces, although the old Free State laws differentiated between him and the Native.
>
> It is high time that his right to vote in Parliamentary elections be admitted by the Northern Provinces, and to deny him this right would be rank injustice. [South Africa, 1967]

Such talk was heady stuff for the sanguine Coloureds. Here, at last, was the word from the great Boer father figure. Integration, certainly, was right around the corner. By the time the Coloured people realized they had been duped, it was too late. The first signs of the true feelings of the Afrikaners for the Coloureds became apparent in 1943 when Smuts first talked about "parallel development." The unmistakable sign came in 1948 when Malan and the Nationalist Party won the general election on the issue of *apartheid*. By 1956, they had passed the Separate Representation Act, which took Coloureds off the common roll. Under this act Coloureds voted for four whites who acted as their special representatives in Parliament. The act also provided for two whites to represent Coloureds in the Cape Provincial Council. Only men were eligible to vote, and the procedure for registration was altered so that applications had to be signed in the presence of specified government officials who were also commissioners of oaths. (White voters are required only to sign their applications in the presence of another voter.) The effect of this procedure was to lower the number of registered Coloured voters from 46,051 in 1948 to 9,839 in 1963. In May 1968 the government sealed the immediate political fate of the Coloured people in an airtight *apartheid* compartment by removing the right of Coloureds to be represented in Parliament. Another bill passed at the same time ended their right to belong to white political parties. Thus, the Coloured people, who had recently lost the right to marry whites, live in white neighborhoods, attend white universities, and attend concerts and plays in mixed audiences, were delivered the *coup de grâce* by the Nationalist Government. As a Coloured intellectual said at the last political meeting with whites he could legally attend, "At least now we know where we stand."

When taking stock of their new situation, most Coloureds I talked to were not so sure where they stood, except that they stood uncomfortably and unpreparedly alone. Traditionally, the Coloured people had relied on the English-speaking United Party who had, in turn, patronized them and used their votes to offset the power of the Afrikaner Nationalists. By 1956, the Coloureds had realized that the United Party was not going to help them. But, instead of organizing among themselves, they switched their support to the Progressives, who, many Coloureds admit, used them to elect Progressive candidates who could not win in white areas. Interestingly, few Coloureds ever supported the only truly multiracial party in South Africa, the Liberals. Most of the basically conservative Coloured people had no interest in parties that included Africans. So reliant were they on whites that they had always shunned even all-Coloured parties.

The basic element of the political culture of the Coloured people is their white bias. They have never accepted that they are a separate group from the whites. Their sole interest is not to be lumped together with the Africans. They are interested in protecting the meager privileges that they hold and which are denied the Africans. Of over one hundred Coloured people I interviewed, only three thought that Coloureds should band together with Africans in a political alliance. All the others, including the few who called themselves "radicals" and "Communists," believed that the goal of the Coloured people should be integration with the whites. For example, after the famous Sharpeville incident in 1960, 30,000 Africans marched on the Town Hall of Cape Town. They had asked the Coloured people to join them in the strike, but the Coloureds flatly refused and stayed at work. The Coloureds seem as intent on holding the line against Africans as the whites are intent on keeping a barrier between themselves and Coloured people.

In defense of this position, Coloureds argue that they must stay with whites because they lack a separate political and economic structure upon which a group identity could be based. Other factors that militate against a community feeling are the lack of strong group myths or traditions and a common ethnic origin. Unification is all the more difficult because of strong class distinctions among the Coloureds and the lack of any territory or land that is exclusively Coloured. Whites live in Woodstock and District Six, two of the most thoroughly Coloured areas in central Cape Town. Even in predominantly Coloured areas, whites control the economy. In District Six, the unofficial Coloured "capital," the estimated market value of properties in 1966 was 17 million rand for those owned by whites and only 6 million rand for those held by Coloureds, even though only 1.3 percent of the population there was white. Coloured property ownership was undoubtedly considerably higher in middle-class Coloured areas of Cape Town, but nowhere did Coloureds come close to controlling their own economies.

The Coloureds are not a self-supporting society economically, nor do they have an integrated culture that is directed toward certain societal goals. The Afrikaners, by contrast, have a culture with a rich historical heritage. They have culture heroes and a panoply of language and religion that lead to national pride. Afrikaners have a self-appointed mission to fulfill in the world—to be the bastion of Western civilization in Africa. The Coloureds have no heroes, have little respect for their language, and are divided along religious lines. Their only goal is the dissolution of their group. It is no wonder, then, that they voted for white candidates (to the exclusion of their own people) for over one hundred years.

Wilson and Mafeje (1963) report that the Xhosa in Cape Town use a derogatory term for the Coloured people, *ilawu*, which means a rogue, someone without customs and traditions who is capable of doing anything immoral. In South Africa, whites and Africans display a sense of solidarity while the Coloureds do not. Some Coloureds say this is because they are so much a part of white society that it is impossible to separate themselves from it to fight it. Therefore, because the Coloureds have accepted and internalized white racial standards, the end effect has been not only an estrangement from other nonwhite groups in South Africa but a loss of self-respect that undercuts any possibility of organization. As the Xhosa say, the Coloureds are people without customs and traditions, people who hate themselves so much that they will not rally behind any specifically "Coloured" banner. Coloureds form few voluntary organizations and follow few leaders. Now that the Coloureds have been cut free from political dependence on whites, and the concomitant illusion of potential integration, they find themselves in need of the communal support that society normally provides. But without a group consciousness, Coloured people complain of being alone, of being individuals in a world of groups.

Ruth Benedict wrote that societies that survive are ones that integrate all their miscellaneous behavior into a consistent pattern. The following review of some aspects of the political behavior of Coloureds may indicate what elements, if any, of a consistent pattern exist. The future of the Coloured people as a group depends on such questions of social integration.

POLITICAL LEADERSHIP

The people of Woodstock have in common with the people of Watts not only a matrifocal family structure but also similarities in political organization. As in Watts, there is no indigenous political structure within the Woodstock Coloured community. Political processes occur outside the community and have long-range effects on the life chances of Woodstock's citizens. The opinions of the people of Woodstock are not solicited by politicians before they make policy decisions. South Africa's national political parties act without the advice or consent of Coloured people. What little indigenous political activity there is in Woodstock is led by a small group of ministers and middle-class individuals. Unlike the women of Watts, however, the women of Woodstock seldom engage in politics. One reason for this lack of participation by women is that middle-class Coloured leaders in Cape Town have been predominantly Moslem and are, therefore, not given to working with women on the basis of political equality—one finds a Mrs. Meir in Israel or a Mrs. Gandhi in India, but one does not find women leaders in Egypt or Pakistan. Women in Woodstock are, nevertheless, active in quasi-political organizations. That they are not political leaders is also due, perhaps, as much to the scarcity of any leaders, male or female, as it is to role differentiation by sex. One prominent exception to this generalization was Cissy Gool, Abdurahman's daughter, who was an important leader in the 1930–1960 period.

In Coloured Cape Town there is an amorphous leadership group composed of the very small middle class of Coloureds. Although 94 percent of the Coloured people are Christians, the minority of Moslems is overrepresented in the middle-class group. They also compose a large—probably over half—portion of the leadership pool. Not all Moslems are wealthy—most are as poor as Coloured Christians —but a significant number stand out from the masses of Coloureds. This is probably because Coloured Moslems, unlike their Christian counterparts, have a bond between them of which they are proud. They have a history of freedom (many of their Javan ancestors came to South Africa originally as political exiles) and their own customs and traditions (such as their food, their unique wedding ceremony, their *Khalifa*, and their choirs). These Moslem Coloureds (often called Malays by whites and 'Slams—from Islam—by Christian Coloureds) make up a large share of the class of nonwhite skilled artisans in Cape Town.

Cape Town's Moslems are among the world's most orthodox, and some still practice female circumcision and polygyny. But they are among the most Western in terms of education, clothing (except for the ever-present fez), housing preferences, and business philosophy. The more affluent Cape Town Moslems charter flights to Mecca. A striking sight at the end of *Ramadan* is the line of Moslems in their new American cars waiting in the predominantly Jewish section of Cape Town (Sea Point) to see the moon in order that they may end their fast.

The mosque is the center of Moslem life in Cape Town. Most Moslems pray at their mosque five times a day—if their employer will allow them the time off. The effect of this discipline is evident in the behavior of middle-class Moslems. Unlike most Coloured people, middle-class members of this minority appear to be free of the low self-esteem in which most Coloureds hold themselves. Some Moslems appear as confident and self-assured as white South Africans. Some consider themselves to be the aristocrats of the Coloured population.

The most prominent Coloured man in Cape Town is not a Moslem, however. In 1967–1968, Dr. R. C. van der Ross was the only man universally acknowledged to be a leader of the Coloured people. He was also, characteristically, one of the most disliked men among Coloureds. Dr. van der Ross was the organizer of the Coloured National Convention which met, despite a government ban, in 1961. One hundred and fifty Coloured leaders met, according to Horrell (1961), and declared that all laws that discriminate on the basis of race should be abolished in South Africa.

The main policy decided upon at the conference was that there was to be no compromise or collaboration with the government in any area of *apartheid*.[1] Little more was heard from the group who attended the conference, but in 1966, when it became evident that the Coloured people were to lose their right to belong to integrated political parties, Dr. van der Ross founded the all-Coloured Labor Party of South Africa to oppose the pro-government Coloured People's Federal Party. But then, as one Coloured man told me, "Van der Ross proved himself to be as spineless as all other Coloured leaders." In 1966, van der Ross unexpectedly resigned the presidency of the Labor Party to take up the post of Assistant Education Planner in the Department of Coloured Affairs. As the Department of Coloured Affairs is the main instrument of *apartheid* directed against the Coloured people, van der Ross was immediately condemned for an apparent compromise and collaboration. "He's a quisling," one man in Woodstock told me. "He was the only one who could lead us," a young woman said, "but now we find him working against our people." Van der Ross, of course, saw his decision in a different light. He explained publicly that he had decided to fight the government from within its own camp and to demand from the government everything they claimed *apartheid* had to offer the Coloured people. Coloureds say that Dr. van der Ross had been called into the Prime Minister's office, where Vorster had said to him, "Dick, we have to bring the whites and Coloureds closer together. And you are the man I've chosen to do it." Publicly, van der Ross said that he couldn't refuse such an offer because Vorster convinced him that the Nationalists would never accept integration; thus, the only way he could help his people, he claimed, was through cooperation with the government. Sympathetic Coloureds explain van der Ross's seeming about-face by saying that his only alternative was political imprisonment on Robben Island. I was often told, "He had no choice. They come to you and say, 'We see you are an influential man among your people. We want to give you a top job. If you don't take it, you will go to jail.'"

The success of the government in incorporating potentially effective Coloured leaders into the *apartheid* system is quite remarkable. George Golding, an anti-

---

[1] The nonracial state to which the convention referred would not, presumably, include Africans. The selective perception of South Africans of all races is legend. We need only recall that when one spoke of race relations in the old Union he meant the interface of Boer and Briton.

government associate of van der Ross in the early 1950s, was persuaded to take the post of chairman of the government-sponsored Union Council for Coloured Affairs. The chairman of the group receives 840 rand while the other members receive from 480 to 650 rand for meeting fifteen days a year. The most recent chairman of the Council, Mr. Tom Swartz, found working for the government so much to his liking that he founded the pro-government Coloured People's Federal Party. In Cape Town, where six of forty town councilors are Coloured, one councillor, a Moslem, said publicly that he favors *apartheid* because he does not feel that Coloured leaders are politically mature enough to sit in Parliament with whites. Another Coloured Capetonian testified to a Parliamentary committee in 1967 in favor of the Coloured people losing their representation in Parliament:

> For a person to go to Parliament he must possess a certain amount of knowledge and a certain amount of brains. We have not reached that stage yet because as I have said earlier on we have always been dependent on the white man. We are only now, stage by stage, finding our feet. We are only now trying to become independent. That is why I say it is of the utmost importance that we must have the guidance of the whites. They must help us and they must educate us. We have not the proper men, the leaders, the debaters to put our case.

Such self-deprecatory remarks do not necessarily alienate a Coloured man from his people. The white bias of the Coloureds runs so deep that only a few intellectuals and radicals would take offense at these comments. Whites, the reference group for the majority of Coloureds, can therefore do no wrong—except deny Coloureds the right to be white. The only issue in Coloured politics is making the Coloureds white. An intelligent Coloured man bragged to me that he had accidentally bumped into former Prime Minister Verwoerd—the architect of *apartheid* —on the street and the Prime Minister had said, "excuse me." As whites do not excuse themselves to nonwhites in South Africa, this was the high point of the man's life. He was, for a moment, a white man. Another intelligent Coloured man told me that he was a member of the Progressive Party "because it is the only way I can associate with whites." Coloureds also want whites to be referees and judges in conflicts between Coloureds. Quite often in other societies a foreigner is acceptable as an adjudicator when a member of the in-group is not, but in Coloured society a white person is considered preferable to a Coloured in any highly valued role, from spouse to president.

It is, however, unfair to characterize the Coloureds as mere fawning sycophants. Their behavior is explicable from a practical viewpoint. Most Coloureds feel that they can only lose from politics. They say that if the Africans should gain control they still would not have freedom and, in fact, they would lose their economic advantage. One Coloured man said to me, "I'd feel more than foolish shouting, 'Africa for the Africans!' I'd feel stupid." If Coloureds wish to preserve their higher status than the Africans, they also must desire the perpetuation of white rule. This is one dilemma the Coloured leader faces. He dare not protest too much. If he becomes truly successful in his opposition to the Republic's three and one-half million whites, he will find himself in opposition to the nation's fourteen million Africans. (Also, because Coloureds feel no racial or cultural affinity with

Africans, there is no real basis for a political alliance of all nonwhites in South Africa.)

Another problem for the Coloured leader is that he finds himself in an intercalary position linking white authority with his poor constituents. As happens to black leaders in Watts, the whites accuse the middle-class leader in Woodstock of lacking influence among his people while his constituents accuse him of selling out. A Woodstock man characterized the politician's plight in this way: "A Coloured leader is like Guy Fawkes. He'll make a hell of a fuss, but when he turns around he won't find anyone following him. Then he'll catch hell from the government."

In all societies it is the role that develops the leader. Since there is no role for a genuine leader in Woodstock, there are no leaders. The only sanctioned leadership role is that of a government apologist. But few people want this role, and no one is capable of defining, or allowed to define, a new role. Most of the problem is due, therefore, to the intersection of Coloured society by white rules. Another problem that would exist even if Coloureds were allowed political independence is the lack of occupational differentiation among Coloureds. As in Watts, there is little status differentiation among the majority of nonwhite men. Therefore, the potential leadership pool in Woodstock is very small.

THE MINISTERS

One of the few differentiated professions in Woodstock, the ministry, does provide a kind of quasi-political leadership group. There are few Messianic or Zionist churches in Woodstock. Unlike Watts, separatist church movements are seldom successful in Woodstock. The reason, again, is the white bias of Coloureds, who want to belong to a "white" church, not to a "Coloured" church. As churches are among the few remaining integrated institutions in South Africa, people in Woodstock take pride in being members of mixed parishes. The "mixing" in Woodstock is mainly symbolic, however. In the most integrated church in the community only about 5 percent of the parishioners are white.

Coloured ministers have, in the past, been among the most outspoken members of their community. This is due, perhaps, to the reluctance of the orthodox Christian Afrikaners to ban a churchman. Like women, churchmen have greater immunity from political reprisal. One Moslem sheik openly criticizes the Nationalist Government, but remains one of the few Coloureds allowed to travel freely outside of South Africa. Cynical Coloureds say that the government permits religious men greater freedom of speech because ministers have so little to say. Realistically, one cannot claim any great effectiveness for any Cape Coloured churchmen. However, the cases of two ministers must be included in any discussion of Coloured politics because they are among the few leaders well known throughout the community.

In 1949, several Coloured ministers met to protest against *apartheid*. Known as the Wynberg Ring, the organization was short-lived and ineffective except that it served as a catalyst for one of the only successful separatist religious movements among the Coloureds. A Dutch Reformed Church minister, whom I shall call the Reverend de Vries, led his congregation away from the mother church on the grounds that the D.R.C. gave his people watered-down "Coloured" catechisms. De Vries' church, a segregated congregation, as are nearly all D.R.C. churches, reconstituted itself as the South African Calvinist Protestant Church. The minister continued to preach a conservative Dutch Reformed gospel to his light-skinned, middle-class parishioners. Acknowledged by many Coloureds as an "outspoken critic of *apartheid*," de Vries is a difficult man to understand. After having interviewed him I came away with the impression that his primary criticism of the government was that it did not accept light-skinned, conservative Coloureds into the ranks of Afrikanerdom.

De Vries, like many Coloureds, clips from the Cape Town papers every story he sees about race. He has an extensive file. His favorite stories are ones that concern Coloured children in white families. The "Smith" and "Jones" families of South Africa are very well known to all Coloureds. They are families with "Mendel's law" children—whites with a black child. "See, they've all got Coloured blood, too," de Vries says. "With this Mrs. Jones, it was the African milkman!"

Like many light-skinned Coloureds, de Vries thinks of himself as white and feels that the law is unjust, not because it keeps Africans or dark Coloureds down, but because it keeps people with predominantly white "blood" in an inferior role.

> We Coloureds are a League of Nations. We're everything from white men to monkeys. We're the missing link. But I can pass as a Jew. Lots of Eastern Europeans and Portuguese are darker than I am. In the Orange Free State, you are either white or black, there is no "Coloured" classification. If you don't look like an African, you're white. If I get into a queue for nonwhites, they say, "This isn't for your kind of Coloured, it's for Kaffirs and *Hotnots*." But we Coloureds are nothing. I'm not white, not black, not yellow. I'm the dirty trick the policeman played on my mother. This Immorality Act is just a way to keep the Coloureds away from the whites, not the whites away from the Coloureds. It's so petty. We died for van Riebeck and we died for the Voortrekkers at Blood River. We fought the Kaffirs for them. We've lived with them, voted with them, married them, and now they put up a wall. That's why all the better Coloureds are going to Canada.

De Vries dislikes the Group Areas Act not because it displaces Coloured people from their homes but because five of his churches in areas declared white were assessed at one quarter of their value. But what is most interesting about de Vries is that many poor Coloureds claim that he is a man dedicated to helping them.

At the other end of the political scale from the D.R.C. is the Anglican Church. In Woodstock, the Anglicans have the only integrated parish. White Anglican ministers and parishioners in Woodstock supply a degree of political leadership to the Coloured people. The Coloured people respect these clergymen, but feel they are a bit "radical." The most radical Coloured clergyman in Cape Town is the Reverend "Maguire," a young, outspoken Anglican priest who has an all-Coloured parish in suburban Cape Town.

Maguire was a member of the African National Congress during the late 1950s and early 1960s. "They didn't want me. 'You're a half-caste,' they said at first," he related to me. But now he has given up any hope of political activity in South Africa. "We have to be like the American Urban League's Whitney Young. We have to build economically." (Whitney Young was without a doubt a capitalist and one of the more conservative black leaders in America, yet to Coloureds—and Maguire is a self-proclaimed Marxist—Young was a radical.)

We're conditioned to be dependent on whites. I know a Coloured plumber who lived in a small town and worked for a white man who sat in an office and sent the plumber out. The white man was not a plumber, yet he took 50 percent of the profits. I asked the plumber why he didn't take all the profits, since he was the only skilled plumber in town. He said, "I couldn't do that." And then the Coloureds always say, "Look how the white man oppresses me." Coloureds won't do anything for themselves. They refuse to donate to charities that help Coloureds. People don't like to be identified with "charity." That's acting "Coloured"—which is bad. The wealthy won't identify with the poor. One middle-class Coloured neighborhood here voted to change its name because it was the same as the adjoining poor Coloured neighborhood. They split the town because they didn't want to be identified with the poor element. When the Cape Peninsula School Feeding Scheme that provided surplus food to children was discontinued for Coloureds and Natives but continued for whites because "they have a different standard of living," white charitable groups took over when the government abdicated. But you'll never see a Coloured donate to the program. And here we have malnutrition. The people eat off the whites' dirt heap. When I ask Coloureds why they don't help their brothers, they say, "Those people aren't like our class, Father."

A Coloured man has one distinction on the African. He can have freehold property. So status is decided through home ownership. A parent will take his sons out of school so they can work to pay for the house. People become slaves to their houses. They have to maintain the distinction between themselves and the "Kaffirs." Also, you have to speak English even if Afrikaans is your first language. And if a Coloured man should become a doctor or a lawyer, Coloureds still go to the white man. They say, "Who does he think he is? He is only a Coloured man just like me."

We need to build leadership and aspiration. But we are forced into being complacent. If you keep your mouth shut, you'll get a passport. People think that I deserve not to get one because I broke the code. I hope *apartheid* gets tougher so we'll quit being so complacent. None of my parishioners has any contact with Africans, and if he did he wouldn't admit it. . . . The whites reward subservience. If you give a Coloured chap a little status or money he'll clam up right away. I talked to a petrol station attendant who was licking a white man's boots saying, "Yes, *baas*, can I polish your windscreen, *baas?*" He acted like a coon. But he got a big tip. I asked him if he wasn't ashamed of himself. He said, "No, sir, it puts bread on my table." I once tried subservience myself when I worked on a train. I found that the more I groveled the bigger my tips were.

Maguire says he has started what he calls the Reconciliatory Movement in South Africa. He believes it is the alternative to violent racial confrontation. He started the movement by dressing in old clothes and driving around Afrikaner Stellenbosch University until he would see a white student thumbing a ride. He would stop, find out where the student was going, and say he was going there too. He would make the student speak English, which he could do better than the student, and then he would switch to Afrikaans. Since all Afrikaners are interested in the Bible, he would talk about it with the student to establish his intellectual superiority. He would stop at the side of the road and say he was hungry and offer to share his picnic lunch. He had only one cup of coffee, which the student would have to share. He would say, "Now what are you going to say to your father? You met a smart

Hotnot and shared his cup?" Maguire claims that a series of such encounters has led to a reconciliatory movement between Coloureds and whites at Stellenbosch.

Most intelligent Coloureds claim that Maguire's movement is only a wishful figment of his imagination. They also do not hold with his views that economic equality will lead to social acceptance in South Africa. Middle-class Coloureds say he is a fool and cite their own low social status despite their wealth as proof. But it is Maguire's outspokenness that has turned most of the community against him. He is not liked by many Coloured people because, as one man put it, "He's too pushy." Another man said that Maguire associates with white "radicals" and therefore gives the cause of the Coloureds a bad reputation. It is significant that Maguire is not as respected in the Coloured community at large as is de Vries.

Thus far, we have discussed politicians and ministers to the extent that they are involved in what is obviously political behavior. But, as in Watts, what real political activity there is in Woodstock is not built on organized party politics but rather on indigenous voluntary associations.

VOLUNTARY ORGANIZATIONS

Political organization is the process of power accumulation and distribution. To speak of politics in Watts and Woodstock is to speak not merely of parties but of all institutions that wield power in the community. The kind of power held by the organizations we consider now is the power to get things done within the community. Woodstock social clubs, sports groups, and gangs have power because they are organized collections of people working toward stated ends. These bodies serve political functions such as group integration and political socialization. That they are not particularly effective in any of these areas is because power is a scarce resource in Woodstock. *Apartheid* laws and the presence of whites in nearly every aspect of social life in Woodstock limit the number of purely Coloured organizations. The economic position of most Coloureds limits the kinds of groups they might join. Among the Coloureds, as in most Western societies, poor people tend to belong to fewer organizations than do middle-class people.

In Woodstock, there is a correlation between income and group membership, with a tendency toward more group affiliations among the better-paid people. Very few Coloureds, and virtually none of the poor, are members of any political party. For the majority of Coloured people, voluntary associations consist of trade unions, social and cultural associations, sport clubs, musical groups, and gangs. Each of these groups will be reviewed with an eye toward how they relate to the political culture of Woodstock.

Unions Except for churches, more Coloureds belong to labor unions than to any other type of organization. In 1966, slightly over 100,000 Coloured people belonged to trade unions in the Republic, and since then the number appears to have been growing annually. Interestingly, over 60 percent of Coloured union members belong to racially mixed unions. In these unions, even when Coloureds predominate numerically, whites are invariably found in leadership positions. In such unions, Coloureds cannot legally strike alongside their fellow white workers even though they are permitted to vote whether or not the union should strike. Such inconsistencies are at the heart of the Coloured man's political dilemma. His position in the mixed unions is made even more confusing by the fact that there are more Coloured women than men in such organizations. In 1966, 27,723 Coloured men and 37,989 Coloured women belonged to mixed unions, while in the same organizations white men outnumbered white women two to one. In this regard, Coloured women have higher political status than Coloured men, for among Coloureds, prestige is measured by how closely one associates with whites and how large a say one has in white organizations. Over half the Coloured men in trade unions are in all-Coloured unions, while over two thirds of Coloured women belong to integrated organizations.

The integrated Trade Union Council of South Africa takes about the same approach to its Coloured members as do the white political parties. In exchange for Coloured loyalty, the Council (which, without Coloured votes, would be only the second largest union body in the country instead of the largest) pays lip service to integration. In fact, the Council has stated that it favors integration of trade unions as the surest way of preventing employers from using nonwhites at low wages to replace white workers. The Coloureds justify their cooperation in this endeavor by saying that the union also tries to prevent Africans from undercutting *them* in the labor market as much as the union helps whites. The main economic advantage of mixed unions is that they get the same wages for all members, thus giving Coloured workers "white" wages. To some Coloureds, this, however, is a moot point. The most important aspect of the mixed unions to the Coloured way of thinking is that they offer an opportunity to work close to whites. For this reason, Coloured union leaders are highly respected in Woodstock. The present leader of the Coloured Labor Party started his career as a union organizer.

Social Organizations   The white bias of Coloureds is evident even in their social and cultural associations. At one extreme is the Coloured Legion, a veterans' organization that yearly pledges its loyalty to the government and its willingness to fight (the Africans) for the whites. In Woodstock, this is a very small group, however, and the white bias of the larger groups is not usually so blatant. But most associations in Woodstock are organized either to meet whites or as forums where Coloureds can act out their cultural whiteness. In the first category are several small literary and debating societies. I went to a meeting of one of these cultural associations that was attended mainly by schoolteachers who shared a belief in Trotskyism. (Many Coloured intellectuals claim to be Marxists, but few advocate the violent overthrow of the government.) The group meets nine times a year to hear "experts" (whites) speak on such subjects as drug addiction and Vietnam.

There were about thirty men and women present at the meeting I attended. The affair was chaired by a man who kept a firm, almost autocratic, grip on the proceedings. When the floor was opened to discussion after the speech, no one challenged or questioned the white "expert." Instead, various members of the audience stood up and delivered attacks on the "racist, imperialist, and capitalist" powers (the United States, England, and Israel). The speakers were circumspect about South Africa and sedulously avoided saying anything that might be construed as seditious. It seemed that the function of the group was to provide a place where whites would have to listen to the veiled grievances of the Coloureds against the government.

The point of bringing the speaker was not to listen to him but to force him to listen to them. In this fashion the Coloureds had found a way of exercising their desire for political expression. The members of the association had found a safe way of telling off whites and inflating their egos. The function of the meeting was to put a white man on equal footing with Coloureds. For a short time they could do what was the prerogative of whites only in South Africa—command a white audience.

Probably the largest Coloured organization in Cape Town, SHAWCO (Student Health and Welfare Centers Organization), is white-financed and white-led. The organization is sponsored by funds donated by white students at the University of Cape Town. SHAWCO provides free medical attention, food, and a child day-care center for poor Coloureds. There is a gymnasium-cum-auditorium for use by sport clubs and social groups. Because it is white-led, SHAWCO is one of the few Coloured organizations in which middle-class and lower-class Coloureds are willing to take part together. Still, class antagonisms tend to enter into activities at SHAWCO. The social club at SHAWCO consists almost exclusively of light-skinned, middle-class Coloureds who dance to out-of-date rock records. While this goes on the dark-skinned poor youths play carom (checkers shot with a billiard cue) and make obscene remarks about the morals of the middle-class girls. Among poor Coloured youths there is a great degree of sex segregation. Entertainment for this class is seldom mixed sexually, so they are uncomfortable at middle-class parties. Middle-class boys, for their part, fear that the lower-class toughs will break up their party and steal their girls. The whites who run the center successfully mediate between the two groups. Indeed, factionalism would destroy SHAWCO if it were not for the whites who keep the peace. Among the dozen or so clubs and amorphous groups who use the facilities of SHAWCO, the only common denominator is the white leadership that is in close touch with all groups.

Of course, there are some groups organized by Coloureds solely for Coloureds, but these groups tend to be small and almost always lack cohesion. Yet among the middle class some purely social clubs are quite successful. These groups are organized to give their members a chance to "play white" for a night. As mentioned earlier, they organize balls, cocktail parties, and braais, where members attempt to act the way they see whites act in films. In Woodstock, there also are several fairly well-organized all-Coloured church groups. (However, one of the best organized of these is run by a white priest.) Several Moslem organizations also appear to have some internal strength. And many, if not most, poor Coloured people in Woodstock are members of burial societies. Several of these burial societies are highly efficient, but they have no social significance beyond being a kind of insurance policy.

As in Watts, the clubs and organizations of Woodstock are bereft of funds, leadership, and purpose and therefore tend to be short-lived. It seems that because of white bias, class conflict, a high rate of migration, poverty, ignorance, and the lack of a tight family structure to give a sense of "belonging" to a group or society, there are few community bonds in Watts or Woodstock upon which to build stable organizations. It might be that social disorganization breeds further social disorganization. It is certainly true in both Watts and Woodstock that poor people from broken families tend not to belong to voluntary associations.

There are certain difficulties inherent in organizing voluntary groups in any society, but among Coloureds it takes an added push. There is an overt, conscious grappling in any Coloured organization to foster loyalty and cohesion. A Coloured group is considered a success merely if it stays together. A common complaint in Woodstock is that "Coloureds always fight among themselves." As in Watts, Coloured organizers in Woodstock tend to stifle free discussion out of fear that anarchy will break out at any meeting.

It seems that the most successful all-Coloured groups in Woodstock are those that are the least political. This is certainly true for sport clubs, some of which are nearly fifty years old. It is impossible to estimate the exact number of such clubs in central Cape Town, but there are at least fifty soccer clubs alone. Some are highly structured, with memberships of nearly two hundred, and can field as many as ten teams on a Saturday afternoon. Others are informal pick-up groups with just enough members for a side. During the week there is usually a meeting to deal with team fitness, attitude, and strategy. Not the least important aspect of these meetings is to insure that everyone shows up for the game on Saturday. At these meetings nearly all but the very small, informal groups use English as their medium of expression —even if 95 percent of their members speak Afrikaans. But these groups are in no way political. They sponsor dances and the inevitable *braais*, but at these occasions politics is a taboo subject. Many clubs have youth teams attached to them. Besides soccer there are rugby, cricket, baseball, and girls' softball clubs. It is not unusual for a man to join a club when he is twelve years old and still be an active participant when he is forty.

Sport clubs are about the only organizations in Woodstock that are not, in some way, political. Even music groups find themselves in the midst of *apartheid* politics. The most prestigious Coloured music association, the EOAN group, had, until 1965, presented musical plays before mixed audiences in Cape Town's City Hall. In that year, the Nationalist Government ruled that central Cape Town was reserved for whites only, thus ending nearly thirty years of mixed performances at the City Hall. The group has continued to perform for all-white audiences. As there are no suitable theaters for nonwhites in Cape Town, this Coloured group is now in the anomalous position of never appearing before Coloured audiences. The EOAN group was founded by whites and is financed by whites. The director of the productions is always a white man, and none of the musical plays, operas, or reviews presented has ever been written by a Coloured man. The Coloured members of the group are middle class. One member complained about the white control of the group. She said of the white man who heads the organization, and who has the reputation of being a liberal, "He knows how to let you know he's white." On the whole, however, most Coloured members gladly accept white leadership no matter how paternalistic it may be, because they realize that without white support there would be no group at all.

The Coon Carnival   The most disreputable musical groups in Cape Town are the Coons. Unlike the EOAN group, the Coons are a genuine part of Cape Coloured

A Coon troupe on parade in Cape Town.

culture. "Coons" is the generic name for dozens of troupes of Coloured men who compete in the annual New Year Coon Carnival. At the carnival, the brown-skinned Coloureds lamp-black their faces and imitate the American Negro minstrels who visited the Cape for Queen Victoria's jubilee in 1887.[2] The Coons dress in flashy red-, white-, and blue-striped silk and satin costumes and straw hats. They strum banjos and sing American and old Dutch songs. Until 1967, they used to do the cakewalk and strut through the streets of District Six and Woodstock, but the government has moved them into a stadium because they created a "traffic nuisance."

The carnival is acknowledged by almost all Coloureds to be the single most important Coloured tradition. Middle-class Coloureds say the show "degrades the Coloured man," but many of them attend the competition and all are very aware of its history and traditions. The attitude of most Europeans is that, in Sheila Patterson's words (1953), the poor Coloureds are "blissfully unaware" that "their own brown skin could in any way be identified with the pitch-black of the 'coon'."

[2] There are several interesting, if not particularly significant, ties between the Coloured people and American Negroes. In 1900, the first African Methodist Episcopal Church in Africa was founded in District Six. In 1904, an American Negro opened a Baptist Church in District Six. Both congregations are still in existence. Most Coloureds are interested in the American Negro's civil rights struggle, but few equate their problems with the Negro's. Coloureds do not identify themselves racially with black Americans, whom they consider to be like the Africans. I was surprised to be asked on several occasions what civil rights problems "Coloured" people had in America. It seems that many Coloureds think that the tripartite racial division of South Africa is a universal phenomenon. But, on the other side of the Atlantic, there is a little confusion also. American music publishers recently denied the EOAN group the right to produce *Porgy and Bess* because Gershwin had stipulated that the folk opera was to be performed by Negroes only. Presumably, the publishers felt that the Coloureds were not black enough to satisfy the conditions of the composer's will.

This commonly held theory is, I believe, quite incorrect and misses much of the meaning of the carnival.

The Coon Carnival is, in part, an exercise in self-mockery. It is also a celebration, indeed the only celebration, of Colouredness. On *Neuwejaar*, the Coons act out the white stereotype of the Coloured people, of "happy-go-lucky-Coloureds," black fools who sing and dance and care not a whit for "proper" behavior. It is the only day of the year when it is acceptable to be Coloured, the only time when the Coloured people do not play white. On New Year's Day the Coloureds act like what they are in the eyes of the whites all year long, "Coons." One Coon member said, "We paint our faces black so *die Boere* can hate us even more." They act out their primary cultural trait, self-hatred, when they prance about under such self-deprecatory banners as "the Mississippi Nigger Minstrels." It is significant that whites judge the competitions between the troupes at the carnival and that most of the paying audience is white. The Coloureds are saying, "Here I am, white man, exactly the way you want me to behave." Most Coloureds claim that they do not enjoy the carnival. The so-called happy-go-lucky Coloureds are so taken with fright before they perform their self-mocking ceremony that they must fortify themselves with *dagga* and liquor before they march.

Of course, the manifest function of the carnival is probably not solely protest. But so many Coloureds spoke of the bittersweet ambivalence of performing that one cannot believe they are "blissfully unaware" that they are making fools of themselves. The Coloureds are masters at saying *Ja, baas* to the whites while stealing from them behind their backs. All Coloured protest is subtle. Since the Coloureds cannot legally show their feelings, they do it through calling attention to their inferiority. For example, many Coloureds were very upset when it appeared that they were being used as the source of spare parts for heart transplants. But to protest in public would have been a foolhardy act. Therefore, instead of openly objecting to the use of their organs, twenty thousand Coloureds appeared at the

*Participation in the Coon Carnival
often begins at an early age.*

funeral in Woodstock of the Coloured man whose heart was used in the second transplant. It was obvious that their mood was not of mourning, but officially it could be said that they were there to pay their respects. One Coloured man shouted to Dr. Barnard, "Don't worry, Chris, we'll keep you supplied with plenty of Coloured hearts." The comment was interpreted in the Afrikaner press as support for continued operations. The Coon Carnival is a similar form of protest. The Coon is saying, "Don't worry, whites, we won't threaten you by acting civilized." Because of the merriment of the carnival, most observers have missed this point. The singing of the Coons is functionally much like the singing of American Negro slaves. It is a veiled form of protest and, just as important, it expresses the hidden desires of the race. The Coon seems to be saying, "I'm smiling through my tears." Minstrels, fools, and clowns are not necessarily happy people. The Coloured poet Adam Small expressed the psychological mood of his people when he wrote bitterly, "The guitar is my cross."

The Coon Carnival is similar in function to witchcraft or theatrical caricature and is like institutions found in other societies that provide outlets for normally suppressed hostilities. Often humor can be used with impunity in these institutionalized events to mock authorities and express what is culturally not allowed. The latent function of the Coon Carnival may be to provide a displaced means of expressing hostility and releasing socially forbidden aggression. If so, the carnival is very much a logical cultural response to the rigid South African system of racial stratification that forbids any direct expression of antagonism.

The organization of the Coon troupes is notable because it follows the pattern of organizational instability found among all Coloured groups. Most important is that the Coon troupes are not as highly organized as they appear. Only a few of them are ongoing entities. Almost all of them must be re-formed each year. Often the troupes are organized by wealthy Moslems, who tend to be behind many of the Coon troupes and gangs in Cape Town. Although the men start practicing in September, a practice session usually draws no more than a third of the troupe. It is significant that it is difficult to get Coloureds to participate in this spectacle— the one thing in South Africa that is definitely theirs.

Gangs   Many Coon members are members of gangs, but members of the same troupe will not necessarily be members of the same gang. There is overlapping, and there are peripheral members of both groups. For example, some middle-class Coloureds participate in Coon troupes. It is difficult to assess precisely how many Coon troupes there are or how many gangs there are at any given time. The lifetime of a gang or a coon troupe is exceptionally short. Informants told me that in Woodstock, for example, there were once thirteen recognizable and identifiable gangs, but a year later there were only three. The Coon troupes are nearly as unstable as the gangs. Gangs are a kind of deviant adaptation to a world controlled by whites. Given that a young, uneducated Coloured man has few, if any, social options but to take to the street, gang membership might be considered to be a rational choice: Gangs offer some territorial coherence to the streets of Woodstock. The street corner society of Woodstock normally tends to be as amorphous as the Coloured group itself. By and large, the street people, known as *skollies* (juvenile delinquents, petty criminals), are individuals who drift from group to group and area to area. The *skollie* roams the streets going from one unstructured meeting to another. Gangs occasionally give some structure to the *skollie's* environment.

Gangs are usually composed of a core group of from ten to twenty-five Coloured youths between the ages of seventeen and twenty-one. But in case of trouble, the gang can call on the help of perhaps another twenty "graduates." In case of war, the numbers of some gangs can swell to one hundred people from the territory where they are based. These people are unofficial members who have some neighborhood loyalty to the gang. But such a show of strength is highly unusual. During the time I was in Cape Town, gang activity was generally in abeyance, with only one war during a six-month period. I talked with a few gang members, and their activities struck me as a substitute for political activity. Theirs was a deviant adaptation to the powerlessness of their situation. Significantly, all the gang members I had contact with had tattooed on their skin the words, "Born to suffer." Hercules is a member of this gang, the Young Guns:

> Hercules is a nineteen-year-old who was born in a tin shanty, a *pondokkie,* to a drunken father and a domineering mother. At an early age he was stabbed with a knife by his father and has often been ejected from his house for long periods by his mother. He first had sexual intercourse at the age of eight. Hercules is a man of the world. He went into a life of crime at the age of eleven when hanging on buses and tormenting the drivers became a childish bore. He has a criminal record—three convictions and a dozen arrests—and has smoked *dagga* since he was ten. He has been a member of the Young Guns since he was fifteen. He has been in several gang wars and gang rapes (of both women and men).
>
> The last leader of the Young Guns "liked to kill people too much," according to Hercules, so he was thrown out of the gang—but without him the gang has begun to dissolve. Still, Hercules' best friends are his fellow gang members who call themselves Bread Cat, Fish, Penis, and Ass Hole. One of his best friends is a Moslem with a lengthy record of arrest whose mother will not allow him to take part in a Coon troupe because "they are a bad influence on boys." Hercules and his friends are in constant battle with the "beetles"—middle-class youths. The Young Guns call themselves "outies"—tough, working-class sorts. The "outies" remove their front teeth "to make kissing and other things better," Hercules says with a grin. The "beetles" look down on the "outies" and their "uncivilized" behavior. This reaction provides the "outies" with an out-group. Thus, the immediate enemy of Hercules and his peers is not whites but middle-class Coloureds.

Were the enemy to be whites, Hercules would probably be in jail. The gang wars and the class wars among young Coloureds are a relatively safe way of releasing aggression. The Young Guns know that it is foolish to make trouble for whites, so that nearly all the crime of the *skollie* is committed against Coloureds. One *skollie* told me he would never try to rob a white man because "they'll hang you if you knife a white man." Coloureds, who by law do not have access to firearms in South Africa, know that a white they attempt to rob may be carrying a pistol. Therefore, Coloured violence is directed against other Coloureds and the consequence is mutual mistrust.

The *Cape Times* publishes daily reports of as many as forty knifings a night in Coloured areas of Cape Town. Nearly every poor Coloured man has been the victim of such violence. One of the few ways a Coloured man has of proving his manhood is violence. Scars from fights and police canings are signs of status in gangs.

The aggressive assertiveness of *skollies* is their way of adapting to their inferior status. Crime, sex, violence, and gambling are the only ways a young Coloured can prove to himself and his peers that he is a man. Such behavior is a kind of compensation for his failures in other fields because it stresses his strengths instead of his weaknesses. The world of the *skollie* is a masculine world that compensates for the power of the woman in the home. His language is replete with manipulative words that stress the power of the male role. "To take advantage" is a phrase used by *skollies* when referring to male-female relationships.

For the *skollie* the advantages of work are marginal. A man can build no capital on his wages, but he can build emotional capital among his friends. As mentioned earlier, the gang is a place for moral support. For the gang member, being a "good fellow"—a jovial conversationalist, a hardy drinker, and a tough fighter—is to have high status in the eyes of one's peers. Such friendship becomes very important in a society where high wages and other signs of upward mobility are regulated by *apartheid* restrictions. Among street men in Woodstock the man with many friends is held in the greatest esteem. Most important, this respect helps to bolster the street man's self-esteem. Such effects of peer networks have been found in many urban slums. However, they are not found to such a large degree in Watts because the geographical spread of the area fosters anonymity rather than a neighborhood feeling. Even in Woodstock, which is very much a neighborhood in the traditional sense of people knowing their neighbors and knowing the territorial limitations of their community, the social networks of street corner men are not quite so fully developed that they serve as a substitute for family, job, and religious institutions.

An important reason for the high level of violence in both Watts and Woodstock is the absence of community social controls. In Woodstock there is a general failure of the societal inhibitions that restrain violence. Every society has its rules of conflict, but Woodstock is not a "society." Since there is little loyalty to the group, a weak kinship system, and no history or traditions to fall back on, there is scant justification for obedience to rules. This is a true anomic situation. The absence of social groups and group identification with race causes the individual in Woodstock to fall back on himself. Weaker individuals living under such conditions will try to compensate through aggressive antisocial behavior or they will retreat from the situation through drugs and alcohol. Almost everyone living in such circumstances suffers a loss of self-esteem because he has no group to identify with and thus must accept all failures as personal weaknesses.

Anomie stems from the inability of an individual or group to achieve the cultural goals of society through institutionalized means. The gangs, Coon troupes, and "play white" clubs of the Coloureds are substitutes for the white institutions of which they long to be a part. The Coloureds suffer alienation because they are within the white social system yet, at important institutional levels, they lie outside the system. They share the values of white society but have a feeling of powerlessness because they are not the masters of their own fate. Coloured people believe they are merely instruments to the machinations and manipulations of others, that their behavior cannot determine the outcomes they seek. Therefore, the aggression of the *skollie* is a reaction to these feelings that stem from a profound sense of personal frustration.

The entire political culture of the Coloureds reflects this sense of powerlessness. Coloureds never talk of being able to change their own political position in South Africa. They always say, "The whites must do it." "Only someone from the outside can solve our problems." One young man told me that the answer was for South Africa "to return to the Commonwealth so we can have someone from Britain be a Governor General." Never do Coloureds say that anything in their lives could improve by some action that they might take unilaterally. Due to this attitude, perhaps more than to the practical unfeasibility of operating in a police state, Coloureds are unable to organize. They believe only the whites have the capability of instrumental action.

An individual's motivation is largely determined by his environment. South African society leads to the defeatist attitude and low level of aspiration of the Coloureds. They anticipate failure. The result is the white bias of the Coloureds: They see themselves as inferiors because they see themselves through the eyes of white society. Here is one source of the failure of Coloured political organizations. Coloureds do not want to be a part of inferior institutions, and a Coloured institution is, by definition, inferior. To Coloureds, that which is good is white. The class conflict among the Coloureds grows from this same root. It is, after all, only the white blood of the Coloureds that gives them justification for maintaining a higher status than the Africans. To be respectable, a Coloured man must look white, act white, and think white. Given this set of imperatives, it is obvious that Coloureds cannot form stable "Coloured" institutions.

The whites in South Africa keep the Coloureds from becoming united by showering compliments and favors on those Coloureds who act white and show disdain for "Coloured" ways. Whites, even liberals and intellectuals, encourage Coloureds who do not "act like Coloureds." The English-speaking political parties in South Africa have always embraced the brown Englishman while displaying considerable prejudice against the masses of Coloured people. Whites recognize two different kinds of Coloured people, "those who live like whites" and "those who don't care and don't try to improve themselves." Indirectly they suggest that one improves oneself the closer one comes to living like a white. White liberals never say anything good about being Coloured when they compliment a nonwhite. They say, rather, how much like a white man he is. This is the core of the dilemma of the people of Watts and Woodstock. They are told that it is of low value to be nonwhite, but they are denied access to the white world.

This dilemma leads to political inactivity, frustration, and confusion among the Coloured group. The resolution of the problem has been for increasing numbers to emigrate to Canada.[3] For those who stay, like the two individuals below, politics is not considered to be the source of resolution. Jacobus and Sam are aware of the political nature of the problems they face as Coloureds in South Africa. Yet, they do not see political solutions.

___

[3] This emigration is significant because almost all those who left were middle-class professional people whom the Coloured group could scarcely afford to lose.

JACOBUS

Jacobus is light-skinned, a printer, the member of a racially mixed union and has a high income for a Coloured man. He speaks English: "Our basic philosophy is 'Thank God we're not black.' Things are bad, but they could be a lot worse. We always say, as long as they don't close the Star Bar,[4] we're all right. The main thing is not to lose the privileges we have. We don't identify at all with the Africans. We try to avoid that. I was a member of a soccer club where the test of admission was if you could pass a pencil through your hair. It's all right for a Coloured woman to be a prostitute for whites, but she's scorned if she marries a black. But if the chips are down, I suppose we'll have to beg the blacks to have us. They hate us, and rightly. The most cruel person to an African is a Coloured who has passed as white. He treats Africans like dirt. And the African doesn't think, 'That's a white man doing that to me.' He thinks, 'That's a scared Coloured man doing that to me.'

"We all hate the whites but we can't organize any opposition. But that doesn't mean opposition isn't there. All of us were hoping Washkansky[5] would die. We hated all the crowing about it in the papers, 'proof of superior Western civilization over black.' Hell, Barnard lives in a house where a Coloured man used to live. He's an Afrikaner and speaks broken English. He's just a mechanic to us.

"Where I work I do the job of a white man but I'm paid half the salary. If I make a mistake my boss says, 'Now, you're a smart Coloured man, that's the kind of mistake an African would make. That wasn't a Coloured mistake!' The Afrikaners are crude and uncouth. Once a Coloured man can afford an education he switches to English. Not because we love the English, but because we hate the Afrikaner. But we have no group feelings and couldn't care less about Pan Africanism. The highest status goal for a Coloured is to be classified white.

"There's nothing I can do about these problems, however. But I can have a nice house, a new car, and fashionable clothes. I concentrate on those things, not on politics."

SAM

Sam, who speaks Afrikaans, is about as poor and as black as a Coloured person can be. He is a lorry driver and the father of eleven. The seven older children are married and he has recently adopted four young children. Once he was interested in sport, but now his life is limited to his job and his family. They live in a three-room house. He has children around because "They make my life. This little one knows me only as his father," he says proudly. He feels that a Coloured man has no chance in the society, that Coloureds are disunited and that all the light-skinned want to do is "pass." He says that the biggest problem with living where he lives is the *skollies* who rob working people on pay day. "You not only have to watch the white man, you have to watch the Coloured man, too." He fears the Africans, but respects them. Being black himself, he showed the greatest desire to work with the Africans of any of the Coloureds I interviewed. He admired Kenyatta and other African leaders, but deplored the violence of black Americans. "We must ask the government for what we want in an orderly way," he says. He feels the police do a good job protecting him

---

[4] A notorious Coloured bar in District Six.
[5] The first heart transplant patient.

and there are many good whites working for the benefit of the Coloureds and other nonwhites. "But I cannot even talk to a white woman on the street without fear. My wife and I went to the zoo with Mary [a white liberal]. My wife fell behind with our child and all the whites were staring at me. I just kept thinking, 'Why doesn't my wife catch up?'

"I would never emigrate to Canada. They can shoot me, but this is still my country. We're too afraid now to talk politics because the Nationalists are so strong. But one day, after I'm dead for sure, this will have to change."

In 1967, a Parliamentary commission concerning the political future of the Coloured people reported that they "have to look to the Whites for guidance and are unfortunately only too easily exploited in the process." The "exploitation" the Nationalist Party commissioners refer to is, of course, the success of the opposition parties in garnering the votes of the Coloureds at the expense of the government. But the commission's finding was correct, nonetheless. It was because the Coloureds had never been permitted to make any important decisions affecting their lives that they were unfamiliar with political processes. Like the people of preriot Watts, the people of Woodstock had a political culture in which the central belief was that they were powerless to direct the course of their own lives. Therefore, neither the people of Woodstock nor those of Watts were able to form effective secondary institutions. No leadership group formed in either community because potential leaders were too concerned with winning a niche in white society. As in Watts, the political structure of Woodstock had been determined by the white social system.

The political culture of the people of Woodstock is similar to that of the people of preriot Watts. Neither group had a real understanding of political processes and both felt alienated from the system. Like the people of Watts, the people of Woodstock knew they were being wronged and knew what they wanted out of the system. But this desire was not enough to secure for them the equality they wanted for the reason that almost all the people of Woodstock were political subjects. Few, if any, were participants. And in a political system it is only the participants, that is, those who are a part of the input processes and of decision-making, who have the power to affect the course of their lives.

Although many, but by no means most, Woodstock people were oriented to such output functions of politics as law and welfare, almost none took part in the input functions of political socialization and interest articulation (placing demands before the government). Coloured people did not take part in governmental processes. Therefore, like Watts, Woodstock was an incomplete community. The personal problems of the people could not be solved through public affairs. This important social link was incomplete because of the incursions of the white social system into the nonwhite community. The alienation, low self-esteem, broken family structure, and political disorganization of Watts and Woodstock resulted from the fact that these communities could not create the power within themselves to change to more satisfactory ways of living.

In the last part of this study I review the creation of power and the uses of group identity as they relate to social change in Watts and Woodstock.

PART THREE | Cultural Nationalism, Power, and Social Change

8 / The new consciousness in Watts

Thus far I have characterized Watts as an anomic community marked by political and family disorganization. This is, I believe, an accurate account of social life in Watts *prior to 1965*. Since 1965, however, there have been increasing signs that the social organization of the community is moving in the direction of the American norm. Although this transition is far from complete, it is safe to say that a new indigenous leadership group has arisen in Watts and that there is now a feeling of community spirit and pride. In Woodstock, too, there have been some significant recent events, and although it is too early to predict the effects they will have on community social structure, it appears that Woodstock may be at the first stage of a change similar to the one taking place in Watts.

In August 1965, Watts erupted in an open rebellion against the Los Angeles Police Department (and later the National Guard). Thirty-three people were killed, all blacks but one, and fire damaged millions of dollars worth of property in the community. The story of the riots has been exhaustively documented, and many studies have been undertaken to uncover the causes and meaning of the rebellion. The causes of the riots usually given are these: There was a history of discontent in the community. The grievances of the people ran from discrimination in housing and jobs to the practices of merchants operating in the community to maltreatment by the police. The problems of poverty led to social unrest and aggression born of frustration. In the absence of legitimate means of expressing grievances, such as genuine political representation, the people of Watts took to the streets on a hot summer day in an unprecedented burst of violence.

If the point of view taken throughout this study is valid—that is, that all parts of a social system are interrelated—then the changes that have taken place in Watts, even the riot, can be explained in terms of other social factors. I would argue, therefore, that the riots and subsequent changes in the social structure of Watts came about, at least in part, as a result of changes that had already occurred in the white community. Concomitantly, blacks had begun to change their attitudes about their role in American society. Their political identity began to change as white society began to liberalize its attitude toward blacks. Blacks began to feel that through unity they could achieve some of the power they had previously thought they were incapable of attaining. They later speeded up this process of power accumulation by applying black power myths to their political situation in Watts. Black power leaders convinced young blacks that their inferiority was only perceived and that they were as capable of political organization as whites. Therein lies the intertwining of cultural nationalism, power, and social change.

Even before the Watts riot the whites in Los Angeles had begun to grant power to the black community. But in the ghetto, the expectations of thoroughgoing improvements that were fostered by well-meaning whites outstripped the society's ability to produce them. For example, the people in Watts believed the rhetoric of the New Frontier. They were confident that their problems would be solved quickly. When change came slowly, the blacks were disappointed and chagrined at being once again fooled by whites. In many ways, the riot was like a "revolution of rising expectations"—conditions were improving in Watts, but not fast enough to keep pace with expectations raised by liberal rhetoric.

It may be posited that minorities convinced of their powerlessness cannot even revolt without some prior enabling action or consent from a powerful majority. The history of the black in America seems to support this case. Whites, not blacks, freed the slaves. Whites, not blacks, were responsible for major civil rights legislation. Whites, not blacks, economically supported such "Negro" organizations as the Urban League and the National Association for the Advancement of Colored People. And it was the actions of whites that enabled the current social revolution to occur. The process started with the Supreme Court school desegregation decision of 1954 and was continued with the Civil Rights Act of 1957 and four subsequent civil rights acts. The liberalization of white leadership gave blacks the confidence and, therefore, the power to begin to act on their own behalf. It is no coincidence that the first civil rights sit-ins began in February 1960, one month after John F. Kennedy took office. The current black power movement is a phenomenon growing out of these earlier actions of whites. Harold Cruse (1967) has noted:

> . . . the black revolutionaries of the 1960's forget that it was the Supreme Court decision of the 1950's that gave initial sanction and set the stage for the new-wave civil rights movement that later became the Black Revolution.

The bloc of black voters was not even responsible for the decision of politicians to pass civil rights legislation. Gunnar Myrdal said that such decisions were fundamentally the resolution of a moral dilemma with its focus in the white man's heart. James Q. Wilson has stated:

> It would be a mistake to assume, for instance, that Kennedy or Johnson pressed for civil rights to get the Negro vote for their party. The Negro vote is too small and too diffuse to overcome the white votes they lose by such a maneuver. Civil Rights Bills come about when large numbers of whites within the party demand them.

Sociologists have noted that political acts change the social structure in a way unplanned by politicians. Certainly, the integrationist Supreme Court of the 1950s did not foresee that its actions would indirectly lead to demands for racial separatism by blacks. The ramifications of the War on Poverty in Watts also illustrate this phenomenon. Prior to the riots, the Office of Economic Opportunity had funneled several million dollars into programs in the Watts area ranging from job training to teen-age clubs. These projects were based on a system of "maximum feasible participation" of ghetto residents—that is, the projects were to be run by the people themselves. This federally sponsored exercise in self-government was the first opportunity most blacks in Watts had ever had to participate in large organizations in which they could set policy and decide how to allocate funds. Because most of the people involved were unprepared to handle the responsibility, the War on Poverty was a considerable failure in its first years in Watts. It was a failure in that it did not achieve its stated goal of substantially increasing the welfare of the community. The disillusion caused by this failure was, in part, responsible for the riot that followed. However, the War on Poverty succeeded in a way unplanned by the federal government, in a way that was probably beneficial to the community in the long run. The exercise in self-government gave a political consciousness to the people of Watts and served as a nurturing ground for potential leaders. It made the people of Watts aware that receiving "grants" from whites would not alone solve their problems. In short, it taught the people of Watts the lesson known by every white community in America: a community must be organized to meet its own demands. The government had poured funds into Watts like water on a smoldering fire. It had attempted to pacify the people and forestall confrontation by making the people grateful for what they had received. The money acted more like fuel than water, however. It increased discontent and gave the people of Watts just enough confidence to stand on their own. Government funding was a political disaster for the administration in power and a new lease on political life for Watts.

The riots hastened the rate of change in Watts and proved that there was no genuine black leadership in the community. No leader started the riot, none knew it was going to occur, and none was able to stop it. The middle-class black leaders who tried to halt the destruction and violence were jeered. After the riots, the community was ready to accept a new leadership and support new groups that would operate under a philosophy of self-help. Before examining these new Watts groups, it will be useful to examine the philosophy upon which they are based. Each group differs in its tactics, but all share the philosophy of "black power."

BLACK POWER

The new "philosophy" of black power, also called black nationalism and black separatism, has a variety of meanings within the ghetto which account for the general confusion among whites and middle-class blacks over what the term signifies. To some black groups, black power means a separate black economy; to others it refers to a separate black political community; to many it holds Marxist connotations. But the common denominator, according to Bayard Rustin (1970), "is simply that blacks must be guided in their actions by a consciousness of themselves as a separate race."

The new philosophy in Watts is based on the observation of black people that they are, to use Malcolm X's description, "sick." "The black man is mentally sick in his cooperative, sheeplike acceptance of the white man's culture," Malcolm X wrote (Haley, 1966). Also he is morally sick because he takes dope, drinks, deserts his family, and hates himself. He is spiritually sick because he has accepted Christianity and its otherworldliness. He is economically sick because he is a consumer, not a producer. He is politically sick because whites use his vote instead of his using his own vote. This diagnosis of Malcolm X has been accepted by virtually all of the young leaders of Watts. They have sworn to overcome class differences among blacks, to end divisive color consciousness, the white bias, self-hatred, and political and economic powerlessness and thus "cure" the community. They wish to build community pride and spirit and demonstrate to whites and blacks alike that blacks are capable of administering their own communities. They seek to build an economic and political power base in Watts.

The two primary methods of achieving these ends are cultural change and conflict. Conflict, the more readily utilized method, is the traditional means by which divided groups coalesce. In effect, one of the primary goals of the black power philosophy in Watts is to make whites into a negative-reference group, that is, to turn the out-group (whites) from a reference group into a target for hostility. To root out the attraction for whites, they are attempting to substitute overt aggression for covert aggression. The difficulty they encounter is, of course, that the people of Watts are deeply involved in white culture and heavily dependent on whites economically, politically, and socially.

Black power leaders have a classic boundary-maintenance problem. They must maintain a line between themselves and others. These young leaders are only half-joking when they propose to build a wall around Watts, and they reserve special vitriol for white liberals whom they see as neutralizing the hatred for whites held by Watts residents. They wish to see the whites as united against them as they hope to be against the whites. White liberals now tend to dilute the validity of such generalizations as "all whites are evil." It is, of course, expedient to hate the adversary with whom one fights.

Central to the philosophy of the young leaders of Watts is that open conflict with whites is the only way of achieving their goals. They cite the failures of civil rights "compromisers" as pitfalls to avoid. The conflict in Watts is occurring on two levels. First, there is the obvious white-black struggle. Second, and perhaps more virulent, is the less open conflict within the community. The black community, according to the Los Angeles Riot Study (Cohen, 1967), is roughly divided into three groups: "militants," "traditionalists" (conservatives), and the "survivalists" (uninvolved). The first two groups are fighting to win the necessary third group in order to form a majority. The militant black power leaders are utilizing methods of conflict against conservative blacks in much the same manner they use conflict against whites. In attempting to close ranks to fight the enemy (the whites), black power reserves its greatest wrath for renegades and such heretics as the conservative "Uncle Toms." Their attitude is much the same as the Kikuyu Mau Mau, who found it necessary to kill countless more of their own people than the real enemy (the British) in order to achieve their ends. Likewise, the new leadership in Watts realizes that without unity it can go nowhere.

The young men of Watts have been remarkably successful in winning middle-class blacks to their cause. Prior to the riots middle-class blacks often displayed considerable disdain for "those other niggers" and attempted ritualistically to avoid anything "black." The greatest success of black power has been the winning over of many formerly antagonistic middle-class blacks to the cause of all black people. Significantly, many of the groups in Watts are headed by middle-class blacks who have moved back into Watts from integrated or middle-class black suburbs. These recent changes in Watts demonstrate the functional aspects of black power conflict for black society. Most studies of social change by anthropologists deal with the degeneration of societies going from "healthy" traditional ways of life to "unhealthy" states caused by the conflicts inherent in culture contact. But conflict can be functional. In the case of Watts, conflict has led to generative social change. Cohesion and solidarity have come out of conflict because of the "harnessing of aggression by culture," in Malinowski's phrase.

By harnessing the radical, that is, structural change, in Watts to a cultural philosophy, the conflict that could have led to further disintegration of the community has led to a remarkable degree of integration. Watts is now more of a community in the traditional sense than one would have imagined possible before the riots. (Of course, it has not yet become a true community, but the indications are overwhelming that it is moving in that direction.) Although the fomenting of hatred of the white man has been a primary conflict method to achieve unity, the promotion of love of the black man has been a more important cultural method to achieve this end. Thus, the creation of a culture in Watts has led to the first steps in solving the problems of political and family disorganization that have been the subjects of this study.

Black power, or black nationalism, is, in the words of E. Essien-Udom (1964), "a search for identity in America." Blacks are trying to create a pride and love of race by asserting their racial identity. They feel they must overcome their preoccupation with white material and cultural norms that they are economically and educationally incapable of attaining. To achieve this end they have embraced the belief that as a group blacks share a common heritage of language,[1] culture, and religion. They believe that their singular ethnic identity and way of life grant them the right to control their own social, economic, and political institutions.

In Watts, some of the applications of cultural means to build identity are very conscious. Perhaps the most explicit such exercise is that which is undertaken at the Mafundi (Swahili for "survival") Institute. The institute is directed, significantly, by a middle-class black who teaches Watts residents to use dance, the theater, and other art forms to act out their new, assertive role in society—to learn, in their words, "how to survive" in the white world. Art and politics are inextricably mixed at the institute, where culture is used studiously as a tool to create a positive political identity for the people in the ghetto.

The assumption upon which this new black philosophy is built is that blacks must define their own image rather than accept their image from whites. In their terms that image is a positive African personality to overcome the negative white stereotype of the black as lazy, apathetic, shiftless, and stupid. The cornerstone of their new image is the African heritage of black Americans. People in Watts now

---

[1] Their "common language" is the ghetto patois spoken by all poor and many middle-class blacks in Los Angeles. Some black nationalists claim that Swahili should become the *lingua franca* of black Americans.

learn Swahili, wear African dress, and refer to themselves as Afro-Americans. They learn the history and political geography of Africa much in the way white Americans study Europe.

Many people in Watts say that seeing Africans seated in the United Nations on equal footing with Europeans bolstered their self-confidence because it belied the myth of white superiority. The timing of the rise of black American pride with the independence of African states is far from coincidental. Until Ghana became a free nation, blacks in America had been ashamed of their ancestors, whom their white reference group thought of as savages. Along with a pride in their African heritage, black Americans have begun to feel that they should have their own standard of beauty. Whites in America have had not only a monopoly on power and money but even of beauty. Now, partially due to the emergence of Africa, there is an African standard of beauty in America's black ghettos. Young people in Watts no longer take the "process" (the painful lye treatment that removes the kinks from a black man's hair and makes him "look white"), nor are they buying skin bleaches. For now "black is beautiful" and the "natural" Afro-American look is in style. This may seem unimportant, but the change symbolizes that black men no longer hate themselves for not being white, that they will no longer rely upon whites. The young black in Watts is not yet entirely proud to be black. He has been told to be ashamed of his blackness for too long to forget so quickly, but he is no longer willing to depend on the white standards. The new philosophy in the ghetto has increased the black man's faith in his own ability to change the course of his life.

Before the 1965 riots, many a man in Watts was content to sulk quietly on a sunny street corner. He accepted his fate by repressing his feelings, or exhibited it by wearing outlandish clothes or through inveterate womanizing in an effort to draw attention to his manliness. He was content to prove his masculinity through a false show that, when he came down from his alcoholic or narcotic cloud, ate at his heart like acid.

Now he shouts, "I can't get a job and it's whitey's fault." Certainly, some blacks never go any further with this change in life-style than street rioting and the easy practice of hurling invectives at the white race. But many are going a step further. They say, "We can't count on whitey so we'll have to do it ourselves." This decision leads many people back to school to learn a skill or a profession, or at least it brings them to the point where they encourage their children to stay in school. "Learning how to beat whitey at his own game" by tricking employers to think they are more qualified than they are is all part of the new approach of young blacks.

Another aspect of the new philosophy is to act out one's bitterness and frustrations instead of repressing them to the point of emasculation. The casting off of centuries of repressed hostility has frightened whites. Ironically, it is frightening even whites who have asked, "Why doesn't the Negro do something to help himself? He should assert himself. He's so lazy."

It is significant that many black power and nationalist groups have laid down puritanical rules concerning sexual behavior, smoking, drinking, personal hygiene, and work habits, emulating the Christian, bourgeois way of life that they repudiate.

The old and the new in Watts. A barbershop offers both hair "processing" and Afro "naturals."

Black power groups, while essentially in conflict with white American society, have nonetheless adopted the Protestant Ethic of the white middle class: Success comes through discipline and hard work. While damning the American Dream, it appears that the new leaders of Watts are pursuing it. Black power also reflects the traditional norms of American society with its insistence that women play subservient roles. (There is, of course, the manifest irony of this change occurring concurrently with the women's liberation movement.) Almost all the leaders of the new groups in Watts are young men (twenty to thirty-five years old). Invariably, they are the dominant, instrumental leaders of their households. Male superiority was an essential theme in an undated edition of a Watts publication in the summer of 1969 called *Nigger Uprising*. The following poem was on the front page of the journal:

> BLACK WOMAN
> BLACK WOMAN
> BETTER WAKE UP
> GET UP
> RISE UP
> AND MOVE
> OUT TH' WAY
> CAUSE GOD'S
> GOIN' TO TAKE OVER
> BLACK WOMAN
> BLACK WOMAN
> GOD'S GOIN' TAKE OVER
> AND SET THINGS RIGHT!!

TAKE THESE MEN
OUTTA WIGS
OUTTA WASHETERIAS
OUTTA BABY SITTIN'
OUTTA LIP SERVICE
OUTTA BODY SERVICE
BLACK WOMAN . . N . . N ! !
AND PUT THEM BACK
AT HIS KNEE
BLACK WOMAN
AT HIS KNEE.

AND THEN HE'S
GOIN' TO MOVE
I SAID MOVE
YOU OUTTA THE WAY
BLACK WOMAN
UNLESS YOU WAKE UP
GET UP
RISE UP
AND MOVE . .
. . NOT YOUR HUSBAND
NOR YOUR CHILDREN
NOR YOUR SUPERVISOR
BUT YOU GOT TO MOVE
TO VIRTUE
TO HUMILITY
TO LOVE ONE ANOTHER
BLACK WOMAN
BLACK WOMAN.

So far no statistics have become available to show that the new values of the community have had an effect on family structure in Watts. It will be important to watch the marital figures for the under-thirty age group in forthcoming censuses. If there is a change, it should be reflected in the figures for this group, composed largely of supporters of the new philosophy. Of course, the feeling in the community has always been that men should rule the home. But the fact that this value was stated by matriarchal leaders was a built-in contradiction. Now, young, respected, male leaders are enunciating this value. This difference might cause a substantial change if the economic factors that made for female dominance also change, and there are some indications that this will happen. First, the trend in American ghettos is for female unemployment to overtake male unemployment due to the decrease in service workers in private households, the traditional domain of the black woman. Second, most job training in Watts has been directed at men. Third, welfare laws have changed and should continue to be changed to the point that they no longer encourage the breaking up of the home. Most important, many young people in Watts now express the importance of home life in the struggle to achieve equality with whites. Still, their desires cannot be fulfilled without changes in employment patterns, an area in which blacks have traditionally had little leverage or influence.

"Soul Food" offered to the "brothers" on Central Avenue in Watts.

SOUL

Without the kind of power needed to make instant, sweeping structural changes in the community, the young militants of Watts have been acting in areas where the lack of financial resources is not such a serious handicap. They have created a cultural ethos—the myth of "soul"—which has gone far to unite the community and prepare it for more important changes which they predict will come. Soul is what is called Negritude in Francophone Africa. It is the essence of being a Negro. It is the "national character" of black people.

The qualities of soul are found in the black's music, food, history, and traditions. The people of Watts say it is the quality of shared experience among all American blacks—some say among all black men everywhere. Some blacks in Watts claim that it can be seen in the way black people laugh. Others say it is the ability to survive under conditions of poverty and oppression. Essentially, soul is an umbrella concept designed to foster unity where none existed before. It is seldom defined in Watts. "You got soul or you ain't," is the way it is often explained. The white man is easily put into a negative reference group by the application of this criterion. The cracker, the grayboy, the honkie, Mr. Charlie, or whitey, as he is variously called, has no soul. He is callous, materialistic, and cold as opposed to sympathetic, spiritualistic, warm, "soulful" black people. According to Ulf Hannerz (1969), the culture of soul sets

> new standards for achievement, proclaiming one's own achievements to be the ideals . . . In the case of "soul," the method is that of idealizing one's own

achievements, proclaiming one's own way of life to be superior . . . Using "soul" rhetoric is a way of convincing others of one's own worth and of their worth; it also serves to persuade the speaker himself.

Soul, therefore, is one method by which blacks are attempting to overcome their self-hatred. That soul is based on a far from tangible culture and some questionable "history" does not detract from the fact that it is fulfilling the function for which it was designed. Black power followers raise their self-esteem by building up the group. They therefore build a group consciousness and their own self-esteem at the same time.

The myth of soul has caused many black people to respect themselves and other black people. Thus it has gone a long way toward solving two of the greatest problems in Watts: self-hatred on the individual level and group divisiveness on the community level. Neighborhood spirit and pride have grown out of this change in the self-evaluation of the people in Watts. Where once it was common to hear one black man refer to another as that "black-ass nigger," young people in Watts now call each other "soul brother" and "soul sister." In the past, attachment to the community was weak because the goal of many Watts people was to break out of the ghetto. Now, with a black culture that is defined as every bit as genuine as white culture, there is a greater loyalty to the group. One theme of black power is that individuals are assimilated but only groups are integrated. Now, the goal is to achieve equality as a group, not one by one as was the case before.

The ethos of soul provides the community with a unity that the people of Watts hope to parlay into political power. The political philosophy of black power is that blacks must organize themselves and their communities to gain control of the politics in the ghetto. In the past blacks had come to believe that only whites were capable of political organization. For this reason, the new black power groups do not have white members. They wish to overcome the stereotype that blacks cannot do things on their own. One black leader in Watts told me, "If there was one white man in our organization, people would believe he was the brains behind it."

NEW ORGANIZATIONS

The black power political organizations in Watts are attempting to change the role of the black from recipient to participant in political decision-making. In so doing black power groups fulfill the traditional political socialization role of secondary institutions in a society in the same fashion as white political community groups. But the special problem these groups face is that, due to their lack of political, social, or economic power outside of their community, they have thus far been unable to partake in the output or governmental functions of society. Black power leaders recognize that for Watts to be a full community its people eventually must participate in such functions.

To accomplish this, the young people of Watts are attempting to become masters of their own environment. White teachers, social workers, policemen, store owners, and politicians have, heretofore, usurped most of the differentiated output-oriented roles in the community. Now, the young nationalists in the community ask for black community control of the schools, the police, the economy, and the politics of Watts. To achieve all this, they have organized self-help groups, political "parties," and cultural organizations. The success records of these groups are spotty, but they have accomplished something that few black groups in Watts had been able to do before the riots: survive without white leadership. These new groups have not been completely successful because the power situation in the community has only partially changed. Blacks are still dependent on the white police, white storekeepers, and white welfare agencies they wish to control.

Even though blacks have failed to gain control of these governmental functions, whites have been alarmed by the rhetoric of black power. "Control" is a word that frightens many whites. Yet, what black Americans are now doing is what every group in the pluralistic American society does: it tries to gain and exercise power. Many observers see black power as akin to white neighborhood organizations: Whites run their schools and police departments in suburbia; now blacks are demanding the same rights in the inner cities.

The difference between white and black control of community organizations is, of course, that blacks, unlike whites, cannot pay the bills. This is the central weakness of black power philosophy. It is a recognized weakness and one that blacks in Watts are trying to correct by establishing black-owned businesses, which are often community run. Black power leaders argue that if blacks, for a start, placed their savings with black financial organizations instead of with white banks, capital accumulation could begin in Watts. They argue that Chinese, Italian, and Jewish Americans came to America without capital but managed to survive and flourish through cooperative effort.

In many ways black power is modeled after the struggle of American Jews. Although many of the new black leaders are outwardly anti-Semitic (mainly because most shops in the ghetto have been owned by Jews and because Jews have been involved in the liberal civil rights organizations that are now anathema to militants), the example of Jewry is often cited as proof that a minority can succeed in America. The "Jew Boy" is the Horatio Alger of the ghetto. In Watts, black power leaders exhort: "See, the Jew Boy doesn't go chasing after blue-eyed women, he's busy learning how to beat the Gentile at his own game," and, "You don't see the Jew Boy investing in cracker banks." These statements indicate that blacks wish not integration with whites on white terms but acceptance as a separate, respected, and equal group—like the Jew in America—and, on that basis, integration. Other ethnic groups in America had and still have organizations designed to represent the interests of their "nationality" in the pluralistic system of the United States. Other groups have fallen back on their "old country" history and their culture to bind them together. Blacks, on the other hand, have been neither members of American society nor members of their own group. Unlike the Jews, they had always tried to "go it alone" as individuals. Blacks, heretofore believers in the American myth of individuality, are now organizing in the way all groups must to survive in a pluralistic social and political system. In effect, blacks have always conformed to the stated values of the society—individualism; now they are trying to conform to what is in fact the reality of the American situation—pluralism.

Many people in Watts are now using their new culture to secure for themselves a place in white America. The obstacles they face are great. They have neither the economic resources nor the organizational skills needed to make basic structural changes in their own community. To gain these resources, they must overcome the debilitating group and self-hatred prevalent among black people. They must overcome the lack of education in the community. They must unite the community behind a set of common goals and values. The new philosophy of black power is a functional response to these obstacles. It encourages thrift, hard work, and sobriety. It encourages strong family ties. It fights against juvenile delinquency. It aims at strengthening self-respect. It teaches blacks to believe they can organize themselves. It helps black businessmen and professionals by encouraging people to "buy black." It offers a culture and heritage that black people can be proud of.

The life chances of the Watts man are inextricably tied to the way he evaluates his group and culture. Ruth Benedict (1934) has written that "culture provides the raw material of which the individual makes his life. If it is meagre, the individual suffers; if it is rich the individual has the chance to rise to his opportunity."

The literature of anthropology is replete with studies that correlate culture and personality. What is happening in Watts is, therefore, of particular interest to anthropologists because it presents the unusual case of the leaders of a people creating a culture in order to change the personality of the group.

Several new social and political groups were organized in Watts after the riots with the basic purpose of unifying the community through building a culture for the people. The ideologies of these groups, however, run from Maoist revolutionary to black capitalist. One of the most militant new groups in Watts is the US cultural organization. US means us (blacks) as opposed to them (whites). The motto of the group is "US is everywhere." The leader of US is Maulana Ron Ndabezitha Everrett Karenga, who shaves his head, wears African clothes, speaks Swahili, and is an academically qualified political scientist. For all his flamboyance, Karenga is the most intellectual black power leader in Watts. He has spelled out the philosophy of black power in a book of political aphorisms modeled on the hortative style of *Quotations from Chairman Mao Tse-Tung*. Karenga is not a Maoist, however, and his socialism is pragmatic rather than ideological. As the following selected quotations demonstrate, Karenga is interested in developing the power of Watts. He would restructure the basic institutions of the community to build its internal strength:

> We're not for isolation but interdependence—but we can't become interdependent unless we have something to offer.
> We must free ourselves culturally before we can succeed politically.
> Nationalism is a belief that Black people in this country make up a cultural Nation.
> Without a culture Negroes are only a set of reactions to white people.
> US is a cultural organization dedicated to the creation, recreation and circulation of Afro-American culture.
> The seven criteria for culture are:
> 1. Mythology
> 2. History
> 3. Social organization

4. Political organization
5. Economic organization
6. Creative motif
7. Ethos

The emphasis on white oppression is no longer sufficient; we must also begin to praise Black achievement.

You cannot have political freedom without an economic base.

We must move on every level possible to get power. If we have to get power talking to the man—let's get it. If we have to get power by making alliances with Africa and Asia—let's get it. We must have an organization that thinks, acts, breathes and sleeps the question of power.

We should not be blamed for talking separation. Racism in America has already decided this. We just want to be separate and powerful, not segregated and powerless.

What makes a woman appealing is femininity and she can't be feminine without being submissive.

We say Male supremacy is based on three things: tradition, acceptance, and reason. (Halisi and Mtume, 1967)

Karenga, then, is attempting to provide a cultural solution to primary problem areas in Watts: economic weakness, political powerlessness, self and group-contempt, and female dominance. Karenga's prime political tool to achieve solutions to these problems is to unite all the various factions in Watts into a single political body. For a brief period from late 1967 to early 1969, a coalition of thirteen groups, ranging from the moderate National Association for the Advancement of Colored People to the radical socialist Black Panthers, formed the Black Congress in Watts. As Karenga's influence grew in the Black Congress, a fissure formed between those who supported his cultural nationalism and those who supported the Panthers' belief that "political power comes out of the barrel of a gun." In February 1969, the crisis came to a head with the slaying of two Black Panthers at the University of California at Los Angeles. Shortly after the slaying, two members of US were arrested on suspicion of murder. The Black Congress came to an end amid bitterness and hostility. One middle-aged man in Watts commented to me, "See, it's the same old trouble. You can't get niggers together."

The failure of the Black Congress may have been due to two factors: (1) it was over-ambitious; and (2) it was premature. It can be argued that no such coalition of white groups would be attempted because it would be doomed to failure, or would simply be unnecessary given the white's access to traditional levers of power. That the Black Congress lasted over a year with such a diverse coalition should be considered a remarkable accomplishment rather than a failure. Given the fact that the political culture of Watts had just begun to show signs of change, it was too soon to attempt the kind of coalition that demanded a considerable amount of community unity.

The break-up of the Black Congress did not immediately detract from Karenga's status in Watts. He has considerable influence throughout the black community and has been particularly successful in organizing young people. Besides the regular members of US, Karenga has organized a youth group, the Simbas, who are a kind of black nationalist Komsomol. Even though Karenga has become involved in the struggle with the Panthers, he has established himself as one of the few young men in Watts capable of organizing and running a group with little white aid. At the time of writing, however, it appeared that Karenga's influence may have begun to wane in Watts because of his involvement in violent altercations.

The Black Panthers are a small group in Watts. Unlike US, they are not an indigenous group. The leadership of the "party" is in Oakland, four hundred miles north of Los Angeles. A chief aim of the Panthers, who wear black leather jackets and berets, is to arm black communities to protect themselves against police harassment. The Panthers are not truly a separatist group. They are a political anomaly in Watts in that they are Maoist revolutionaries who believe in a class rather than a race struggle. They have an alliance with left wing radical white groups who are anathema to the other black power groups in the community. The Panthers' chief appeal has been to the truly disaffected and the few Communists in Watts, and for this reason they have far less influence throughout the breadth of the community than the other organizations we are considering.

With the demise of the Black Congress the black power groups split into two factions, the moderate Los Angeles Brotherhood Crusade and the small, militant Black Alternative. The Brotherhood Crusade was headed by the former chairman of the Black Congress. It hopes to raise three million dollars to "improve social, psychological, educational, and economic conditions within the black community," according to their leader. The program includes the founding of a "Black Experimental College" and a family center, designed to strengthen the family by providing legal and medical services and a child day-care center. Also included are "programs to develop and organize the ghetto community . . . programs to publicize, dignify and protect Black citizens . . . and programs to develop and emphasize the arts and capabilities of the Black community." The Crusade is supported by most of the groups in Watts except those allied with the Black Alternative. The Black Alternative is a coalition of several of the smallest, most radical groups in Watts. In 1969, the group appeared to be headed by Mrs. Margaret Wright, one of the few older women leaders active in the black power movement. Mrs. Wright's group, the United Council, is a member of the rather unstructured coalition along with the Black Youth Alliance (high school students), the Student Non-Violent Coordinating Committee (a branch of the association founded by Stokely Carmichael), the Afro-American Association, the Malcolm X Foundation, the Black Teachers Association, and the New Republic of Africa. None of the latter groups could claim more than a dozen members and most are organizations in name only.

Most white observers tend to concentrate on the factional disputes among the black groups and fail to see the constructive aspects of black power that characterize the movement. One of the most constructive groups in Watts is Operation Bootstrap, a self-help organization run by a former director of the civil rights-oriented Congress of Racial Equality, Lou Smith, who is now a black power man. He is a middle-class black who gave up a job in a white company to move back into the ghetto "to work with my people." He typifies the new *noblesse oblige* among middle-class blacks towards the lower class.

In 1966, the group purchased a dilapidated warehouse, installed plumbing, rewired it, and divided it into classrooms. With only one paid employee, a secretary, the group borrowed and begged the necessary materials to remake the old building. Within the first year and a half they had trained several dozen people for skilled jobs. One of their most successful programs has been a dress shop where Bootstrap graduates design, sew, and sell their own products. The group has planned a chain of such shops all across the ten-mile long Los Angeles ghetto. Smith said in 1967:

> This is what black power really is. We have to help ourselves. Most so-called black power has just been rhetoric so far. But the young people don't need to be told how bad off they are or what a devil whitey is, they already know that. Black power has to move from talk to programs. Most black power is just to see who can throw the biggest rally. We've gone a step further. On a voluntary basis, the people in the community who have skills are teaching the unskilled.

To Lou Smith, black power is both cooperation between black people and pride in their being black:

> Black people have one problem in common, we're all in trouble. But white people don't have anything in common. They sit in their private backyards hating the guy next door because he's a Democrat and hating themselves because they lead meaningless lives and hold meaningless jobs. That's what the hippies are complaining about. We don't want black children to have to act like hippies. Black power will prevent that.

Smith believes that eventually the blacks will build themselves up by way of their own "power" to where they are on a par economically with whites. "Then you can have integration," he says. "Until then, I worry about this thing in America that keeps telling us that 'black' is no good. If we were to call it 'colored people's power' or 'Negro power' nobody would care what we did."

Smith says that the prime problem whites have is that

> They are incapable of particularizing when it comes to race. Take Adolph Hitler as an example. Hitler was white, but when he started his mass killings white Americans got on the bus and sat down next to other whites without fear that the stranger may think like Hitler, or be like Hitler, or be a Hitler sympathizer or perhaps even be Hitler himself. But when one black man rapes a white woman, every black man is suspect. A white woman gets on the bus and fears that the black man that she sits next to is a potential rapist if not the rapist himself.

Because of this quality of whites, Smith feels that America has a "white problem not a Negro problem." To overcome this, Smith invited whites to come to Bootstrap headquarters once a week for sensitivity training. Smith dramatically built these meetings into a confrontation between blacks and whites; then he defused the situation by skillfully analyzing the hatred and fears of both sides. "It won't do us any good to build up the black community if the whites remain racist," he says, "therefore we have to educate the whites along with the blacks." Much of the help Smith has received at Bootstrap has come from whites. No matter what is contained in the rhetoric of black power, major undertakings in the ghetto must be made with white money and aid. Bootstrap's largest project, a doll factory, was fully financed by a white firm.[2] Significantly, the black doll made by Bootstrap is popular in the ghetto where black children previously had difficulty obtaining other than white dolls to play with, a situation which may have affected their self-image.

White financing is important to almost every black power group. One new black group, the Watts Labor Community Action Committee, relies completely on white funds. The head of the WLCAC is union organizer Ted Watkins, a burly former auto worker who, according to many people in Watts, is a father figure for thousands of fatherless children in the community. Watkins is an environmental determinist who has solicited funds and materials from unions, government agencies, private corporations, and even movie companies in order to beautify Watts. He has hired thousands of teen-age youths to build vest-pocket playgrounds, plant trees, and clean lots. He has also leased a twenty-five-block-long strip of land that runs under utility poles which he has turned into modern-day Victory Gardens by putting immigrants from the South with rural backgrounds to work growing fresh fruits and vegetables for the vitamin-starved community. His goal is to foster community spirit and pride—and eventually leadership—by involving the youth of Watts in neighborhood projects from which they all reap benefits. Watkins takes over two thousand Watts youngsters to a free summer camp every year and has established an antipoverty work training program for approximately five hundred youths at the camp during the winter. Watkins is another middle-class black who, like Lou Smith, left a comfortable job in the white world to devote himself to the rebuilding of the community. "It's up to the community to supply its own leadership," he says, "you can't leave the ghetto once you've accomplished something." Watkins does not preach race hatred. He believes in building community pride through communal work efforts. He says that before the riots young people were ashamed of being from Watts. Now, his well-disciplined Community Conservation Corps members chant

> Everywhere we go-o,
> People want to know-o,
> Where we come from,
> We're from Watts,
> Mighty, Mighty Watts.

As they sing, they wave three fingers, making the W-sign of a Watts resident. This new pride in Watts comes partly from the notoriety the area received during the riots, but more basically it appears to emanate from a new spirit—what was once just a geographical entity is now on its way to becoming a community. The change in spirit among the young and militant has even prompted the older, more conservative people into self-help action. Thirty-five organizations in Watts that formerly were active only as social clubs have recently united into the Council of Community Clubs. They are now active in the struggle to increase employment in Watts and have thrown their support behind Operation Breadbasket, a boycott of

[2] White money has been very important to black power groups, who have learned how to denounce whites in public and solicit funds in a politic fashion in private. For example, the black Green Power Foundation borrowed $50,000 from the telephone company to finance the "California Golden Oaks Products Company" which makes Watts Walloper baseball bats.

white-owned stores in Watts which have only a token number of black employees.[3] The change in Watts is also noticeable in the more traditional groups such as the Urban League. Recently the Urban League changed its tactics from directly soliciting aid solely from whites to trying to involve the black community itself in the fund-raising process. In 1969, the Urban League sponsored a football game between two all-black colleges from the South. A predominantly black audience of nearly seventy thousand Los Angelenos paid more than $300,000 to see the game. The significant aspect of the game was that it had across-the-board support in Watts. This is the first time the Urban League had enjoyed such popularity among poor and militant blacks. It was also the first time the Urban League had made a direct appeal for funds to the community it was attempting to help.

The new-found pride in the community is probably best exemplified by the annual Watts Festival. The first festival was held one year after the riots to com-memorate the uprising in a constructive fashion. Organized by a group of remark-able young men, all in their early twenties and all residents of Watts, the first festival and the succeeding three were violence-free despite the presence of thou-sands of white tourists in the area. The event includes a Miss Watts beauty contest, a parade, and a festival of poetry, painting, sculpture, and music.

During its first two years, the festival was policed by the Community Alert Patrol, a kind of vigilante group organized after the riots to follow the Los Angeles Police and to report any infringement of citizens' rights by arresting officers. Many of the members of the patrol had taken part in the riots and quite a number were former gang members. The CAP was effective in policing the festival and avoided serious conflict with the regular police. Like other black power groups, the CAP helped, at least in the beginning, to turn former Molotov-cocktail throwers into constructive members of society. There was no magic formula for their success. The new groups merely filled a void by providing needed secondary institutions in Watts.

Black power groups are, I believe, traditional American secondary institutions. The history of communities in America is one of volunteer organizations coming together at times of crisis to meet outside power threats. White communities are constantly banding together to organize school districts, or to petition states for new roads, or to fight federal decisions to locate nuclear missile sites in their com-munities. These organizations are crisis-oriented. The new groups in Watts are fundamentally no different. The following are excerpts from the "Liberation Plat-form," a mimeographed sheet published in 1969 by the Black Political Liberation Organization of Watts. By keeping the demands as they are, but imagining that they were coming from a white suburban community rather than from black and Mexican-American slums, one could come to the conclusion that black power is conceptually no different from the kind of power that whites now enjoy. They demand:

[3] In March 1969, many blacks boycotted the Los Angeles public schools in an effort to gain concessions that would lead to greater community control of the schools. The effort was only partially successful as the community was not as united as it was to be six months later in the supermarket boycott. The nature of the issues admittedly was different, but there is no doubt that the community leaders' organizational skill had improved.

Economy

The establishment of business improvement corporations in black and brown communities.

This agency would be staffed by black and brown indigents and shall be responsible for the over-all economic development of black and brown communities. Presently, black and brown residents own approximately three percent (3%) of the businesses in their neighborhoods throughout the ghettos and barrios of this nation. Through the development of black and brown corporations the agency will serve as a lobby force for satellite industrial complexes through the passage of tax incentive legislation and contract agreements that provide job training, counseling and placement service thereby creating employment opportunities for black and brown people in the development of our communities. Independent black and brown financial institutions must be established so that we will be able to enhance our economic development through our own resources.

Housing

The creation of community development associations in ghettos and barrios so that we may have self-determination in the neighborhood development projects such as the one hundred (100) Model Cities Project.

This agency will also serve as a lobby force for federal and private funds designed to create long term, low interest loans for the purpose of land acquisition for black and brown people. We must own land in order to insure a sound economic base for the creation of housing, business and farm ownership.

Education

There must be massive reforms in the present education system as it relates to ghettos and barrios, if this nation is to remain a productive nation.

Local Boards of Education in urban areas must be de-centralized thereby creating community boards of education in areas with population in excess of one hundred thousand (100,000). Regional occupation centers are needed to provide the necessary job training for those black and brown students who have been the victims of the inadequacies in the present school system. Funds must be dispensed on the basis of population density as opposed to average daily attendance, so that black and brown students can be assured an adequate education.

A national curricular committee must be established to assure black and brown students receiving their history and culture in proper perspective.

Police

Law and order, as it exists in this country, is merely demagoguery and racism. The police force must be controlled by the community in which it is to serve and protect. Therefore, we must have black and brown police forces in the ghettos and barrios.

Redistribution of Power

The development of a black and brown community congress, elected from the community to serve two-year terms through special community elections supervised by local government through the normal election process.

The elected body will present black and brown needs to every level of government as an ombudsman body to the grass roots. Additionally, this body will monitor commissions, bureaus and committees, at all levels of government, federal, state, city and county.

These demands at first appear revolutionary because they are couched in terms of black political liberation. But on close scrutiny, they can be seen as functional responses to the problems that plague the community. The following is a partial list of black power organizations that have sprung up in Watts since the riots. The titles of the groups go far toward explaining the functional political aspects of the new philosophy in Watts.

Self-Leadership for All Nationalities Today
Action Committee on the Urban Crisis
Police Malpractice Complaint Center
Afro-American Cultural Association
Black Man's Self-Image Development Institute
Community Pride, Inc.
Sons of Watts
Watts-Compton Improvement Association
Young Men and Women for Total Democracy
Image Development
Opportunity Workshop
Men of Tomorrow

Almost all of these groups are headed by dark-skinned residents of Watts. Representative of this group is Tommy Jacquette, head of Self-Leadership for All Nationalities Today. A young native of Watts, he speaks the patois of the low-rider. His peers respect him as a legitimate leader, a first among equals. He has worked for the Westminster Neighborhood Association as a director of a project that paid youngsters a small wage to attend a job-training program. Unlike the elected officials in Watts, Jacquette is directly identified with projects that have helped the people of the community to help themselves. Unlike Jacquette, the first elected officials from the area, Mervin Dymally, Gus Hawkins, and Billy Mills, were light-skinned, middle-class blacks who lived far from the ghetto core they represented. Now, the political changes in Watts run so deep that even these politicians must accommodate themselves to black power if they wish to stay in office. I interviewed a black politician who was infamous in Watts for what the community felt was "selling out" to white politicians. This politician had based his career on fighting militants in Watts. He told me that he still did not agree with black power and that it was not representative of the feeling of the majority of blacks. Yet, as the following quotation demonstrates, he had started to develop a grudging acknowledgment of its accomplishments in 1967:

> The black power groups offer a vehicle for frustrated youths to vent their hostilities vocally instead of violently. They present an outlet, an alternative to rioting. If the community is angry with a particular cop, they'll get together with black nationalists and scream like hell and organize a rally and draw up a petition, but they probably won't riot. It's the unorganized who cause riots. The black power people may say things that we can't accept, but you have to recognize them in a free society.

He feels that the secret of the success of the black power leaders is that "They represent their constituency. They come from the ghetto, are a part of the group. They speak the language of the ghetto." This politician sees a difference between this movement and the civil rights movement in the audience that the leaders are addressing:

> Roy Wilkins is talking to whites when he speaks publicly. He is trying to project the image of the N.A.A.C.P. and bring the white community around to its way of thinking. Black power leaders are not speaking to whites. They're attempting to inspire their people. They say, "To hell with the white man" and they really mean it. They say, "The white man stole the civil rights movement, President Johnson stole 'We Shall Overcome,' but let them try to steal the concept of black power."

He feels that the black nationalists are appealing mainly to the fifteen to twenty-five age group: "Karenga doesn't have much appeal to a fifty-year-old." He says that the antiwhite aspect is only a slight part of the black power movement: "What I hear them talking about is self-determination—black people should have control over the economy, police, and schools of their own neighborhoods. They stress self-reliance."

This politician says that he cannot estimate the number of adherents to black power in Watts, but he warns that "You lose sight of the issue if you talk in terms of membership. You have to try to measure effectiveness. Most black power groups don't even have a membership, *per se*. They are interested in influence. When they want a meeting of the 'membership,' they announce a public rally and they hold an open vote."

This politician's comments are significant not merely because they are a considered and accurate account of black power but also because they come from a man who has a reputation for being an "Uncle Tom." That now he would and could be so sympathetic to the movement is an indication of how extensive the changes in Watts are. This politician knows that his constituency will be lost to him if he does not radicalize his stand. He is now operating in an environment that will no longer accept black leaders appointed by the white community, as the following excerpt from a Watts newspaper, the *Los Angeles Herald Dispatch* (September 1969), demonstrates:

> The fight is not against the Caucasian; at this moment, our fight is against our local "nigger leadership." As long as the black people continue to drag each other in the gutter, we'll never be able to move out of the mud ourselves. Our fight must be directed against that "nigger Uncle Tom Sellout leadership." And only when we unite in the community against these people, drive them all the way into the Pacific Ocean, will we be able to see the real enemy.

Again, we must separate the rhetoric of black power from the reality. Black American culture is far more oral than white culture. Bombast and didacticism are part of the spoken—and now written—heritage of the people. This is a legacy from the not too distant past when the only public spokesman for the community was the preacher. Black listeners know how to separate the dramatic chaff from the practical wheat of public statements. (This is partially why whites are so frightened by black power—they have listened to the shouting and not to the logic of the speakers.) In Watts I found that the black leaders who were vehemently antiwhite in their public postures were almost always friendly and helpful to me in private. One leader told me that there is only one style of speech that will reach the black masses and he knew that it frightened whites. "It might be a good thing if they were frightened a bit," he said. Certainly, the fright caused by the riots set fantastic forces to action in Los Angeles. Where previous black leadership had been unable to gain anything for Watts from white politicians, the riots frightened whites into building the new Martin Luther King Hospital, an industrial park, a shopping center, and a neighborhood center in Watts. The conflict seemed to change the norms and values not only of blacks but also of whites.

Moderate leaders now admit that black power has made their job much easier. "Whites listen to us now. They're afraid of the black power bunch and want to shore up our position by granting concessions," one traditional leader told me. Young black leaders are aware of this and take concealed pride in their power to make their more conservative elders more effective. This became clear during the June 1969 mayoral election in which a black city councilman, Thomas Bradley, ran against white incumbent Sam Yorty. Bradley, a former policeman, was not a resident of the poor, central black ghetto. He was, at fifty-two years of age, out of touch with the new young leadership by virtue of both his residence and his age. Still, black power leaders remained silent throughout his campaign. A political leader in Watts explained to me, "We decided that if Karenga or some of the others were to say anything at all good about Bradley, that would have been the kiss of death as far as the white community was concerned. On the other hand, if they had come out against him, it would have split the black community. So we all begged them to keep out of it, which they did." A militant leader told me, "I didn't like Bradley, but I worked like hell for him." A young militant said "He may have been the Jewish candidate, but he's still a brother." Bradley lost, but he succeeded in bringing black Los Angeles together for the first time in its history. Bradley's candidacy and his narrow defeat (53 percent to 47 percent) are symbolic of the changes in Watts. For one, many whites were willing to vote for a black man. This is, in part at least, because of the attention the riots brought to the plight of the black man. It is due even more to the respect blacks have won in the eyes of whites now that they are willing to stand on their own feet. There has been, of course, the predictable amount of white backlash. But the memory of the riots was still fresh in the minds of many white people at the time of the election. Bradley lost, but a political future for the people of Watts may have been won.

9 / Cape Coloured power?

The comparative method used throughout this study is extremely valuable as a tool for weighing the political and social efficacy of black power. Viewed in one light, black power appears to be only an ideology of hate based on myth. However, if we compare Woodstock to Watts, we see a void in the political culture of the Coloured people that, given their problems, a brown power myth might help to solve.

The political and social changes that took place in Woodstock during the 1960–1970 decade could lead to a radical community realignment of the type that has come about in Watts. These changes include the removal of the Coloured representatives from the South African Parliament, the law prohibiting nonwhites from belonging to white political parties, the order banning Coloureds from living in central Cape Town, and, finally, the establishment of an all-Coloured "Parliament." These and other actions were designed by the Nationalist Government to effect the complete separation of whites and Coloureds in South Africa. White politicians in South Africa are insisting that Coloureds stand by themselves politically, economically, socially, and culturally. Whites are pushing Coloureds to develop their own economic base. Whites have legislated that Coloureds will control the internal political affairs of their own communities. Whites have insisted that to achieve these ends Coloureds must develop a group-consciousness based on a pride in their unique culture. In effect, white South Africans—rhetorically, at least—are demanding that Coloureds conform to a philosophy strikingly similar to that of black power. The Coloureds have resisted these changes, but in 1969 it began to appear that against their will they would be forced to stand as a separate political and social group in South Africa. A central question now becomes: If the Coloureds have resigned themselves to being a separate group, as there are now some indications, will they be able to develop—as blacks in Watts have begun to do—self- and group-pride and a leadership class? Because South African society is considerably less dynamic than American society, the answers to these questions may be years in coming, but we can outline some possibilities from the facts we have in hand concerning both Watts and Woodstock.

When the Nationalist Government came to power in South Africa in 1948, it began the slow implementation of its *apartheid* philosophy. Breaking the past promises of Hertzog and other Afrikaner leaders, the Nationalists announced that they were planning separate development not only for Africans and Asians, as had been previously stated, but for Coloureds as well. In 1961, Prime Minister Verwoerd addressed himself to the future of the Coloured people:

> The problem of giving political rights to the Coloureds . . . exists. In this case I accept the rejection of the old proposition that one cannot have a state within a state. I accept firstly that in our State we will have to give the Coloureds opportunities for development, firstly by means of their own local governments, secondly by way of managing the sort of thing now falling under the control of the Provincial Councils—*viz* their own municipal affairs, the education of their own children and similar matters.
>
> Thirdly, I accept that within the White state . . . an institution should be established or a method should be evolved to give the Coloureds further rights of self-government over their national interests. (Horrell, 1961)

On September 24, 1969, the process of politically separating whites and Coloureds in South Africa reached a climax with the election of the first Coloured Persons' Representative Council. Nearly 600,000 Coloureds voted for forty representatives to sit in a council that has limited powers to administer their local government, education, and welfare. The chamber has sixty seats, twenty filled by government nomination. Martin Arendse's anti*apartheid* Labor Party won twenty-six of the forty elected seats. Tom Swartz's Federal Party, which supports *apartheid* with some reservations, won twelve seats. The government used its appointive powers to give the Federal Party and its small pro*apartheid* ally, the National Coloured People's Party, a slim majority in the house. It is notable that only 25 percent of the registered electorate in Woodstock voted in the election—most for the Labor Party. Another interesting fact is the success of several Coloured women in the election—there is a higher proportion of women in the Council than there is in the White Parliament.

Most Coloureds consider the council a sham, since the government controls the allocation of all of the council's funds and has the right to appoint its chairman. Furthermore, the council may not become a viable institution, since the Labor Party candidates ran on the platform that the Coloureds' rights to sit in the South African Parliament must be restored. In effect, a vote for the Labor Party was a vote against the council. It remains to be seen whether the Labor Party will continue to participate in the council and thus give it some legitimacy. Many Coloureds believe that it should. These people say that with the Coloureds' ability to use irony and cunning, the council will appear respectable while actually being an anti*apartheid* instrument. Some Coloureds even claim that the Federal Party is actually the best vehicle by which to connive against the government. "You see," one Coloured man told me, "*die Boere* are very simple people. You tell them that you support them and from that time on they're blind to all your chicanery."

A central question is whether the new council will be used as a tool to gain white status for Coloureds or whether it will become a means by which the Coloureds can come together as a unified group. If the past history of the Coloured people can be taken as a guide, it is probable that even the bitterness engendered by the recent segregation legislation will not cause them to abandon their white bias. It is possible, however, that as the government closes the last doors to integration, the Coloureds will be forced to cooperate among themselves, if only for lack of an alternative.

One of the greatest stumbling blocks to group unification among the Coloureds is their lack of a national territory. Although Cape Town is the spiritual home of the Coloured people, there is no area except for the District Six-Woodstock-Salt River contiguous neighborhood that is historically Coloured. Now, under the Group Areas Act, the inhabitants of District Six, and eventually those of Woodstock and Salt River, will be moved miles away to make Cape Town an all-white city. The Coloureds will lose their architecturally unique homes in the beautiful setting between Table Mountain and Table Bay and will be forced to live in jerry-built government townships on a sand flat many miles from central Cape Town. Although all the Coloureds consider this human removal humiliating at best and robbery at worst, there are some young militants who foresee that the government's plan will backfire. "In Cape Town, we thought of ourselves as Capetonians," a young man told me. "Whites lived in District Six and Woodstock and Coloureds were scattered throughout the white neighborhoods. Now only Coloureds will be in one horrible slum. This will prove to my dense people once and for all where we stand in this country. The Sand Flats are natural breeding grounds for a revolution." This young man may be a bit premature in his speculations. After all, the Watts riots were a revolution of rising expectations. Black Americans did not attack whites until the whites had already started making concessions to them. In Cape Town, where the Coloureds feel their position deteriorating, it is not unnatural that they are in a conservative mood. But the segregating of the Coloured people into all-Coloured townships will no doubt increase their bitterness toward whites and foster group feelings in the long run.

Such *apartheid* measures as forcing the Coloureds together into a separate political, residential, and economic group, although intended to promote the well-being of the white group, may make an unintended contribution to the Coloureds. If the Coloureds are given a separate parliament, separate schools, separate townships, and separate laws, the Coloureds might, in a classic case of self-fulfilling prophecy, become the distinct and separate group they are incorrectly accused of being. The whites may thus unintentionally cure the self-hatred of the Coloureds. They may also unwittingly create another enemy within their own boundaries, but that is not our concern here. Indeed, several competent observers now feel that civil rights has already replaced integration as the prime political goal of the Coloureds.

Will *apartheid* cause the Coloured people to think "Coloured"? The truth is that, like black Americans, Coloureds will think positively of their own people only when there is some kind of history and culture with which they can proudly identify. So long as the people of Watts had only white history and values to which to appeal, they made little progress toward self-reliance; but when they adopted their own values they progressed. It is interesting that white South Africans are encouraging the Coloureds to create their own literature and other cultural media. The Coloured people need their own culture, a history filled with heroes and other forms of collective representations. Black Americans have invented a history that glorifies their slave ancestors (claiming quite mythically that they were nearly always at the point of rebellion). As yet the Coloureds have no such myths. Coloureds may build upon their unique language, food, and customs (their Coons, their Moslem Khalifa), to build their group pride. That they have not already done so is probably due, in Claude Lévi-Strauss' words, to the fact that "Caste naturalizes a true culture falsely." Because of his white bias, the Coloured man has been unable to articulate his Colouredness except when he is in black face and acting the role of the Coon. Coloureds have not yet said, as blacks have, that black skin is as beautiful as white skin.[1]

Yet, Coloured culture contains the seeds of racial pride. Coloureds will claim that they are more hospitable, more musical, and have a better sense of humor than whites. This feeling cuts across the class and color lines within the group and may indicate that there is some common ground upon which racial pride can be built. Certainly, there are very few, if any, Coloureds who find anything functional in their self-hatred. Almost all Coloureds admire Africans for their unity, strength, and stoicism.

Perhaps the *apartheid* laws will have the functional effect of focusing conflict from within the Coloured group to without and against the whites. Perhaps the Group Areas Act will overcome the present drawback of the Coloured population being too geographically divided to organize. Perhaps the class and color hostility among Coloureds will disappear when they are working together in their own parliament. Perhaps economic separation will restore men to the instrumental role in poor Coloured homes. Perhaps the evils of *apartheid* will not, in the short term, be worse than the degrading evils of *baaskap*. It would certainly be ironic if the system designed to permanently subjugate the Coloured people actually led to their emancipation. For the Coloureds, when left to their own devices, have managed to thrive in South Africa. For example, the one hundred Coloured fisherman families of Kalk Bay on the Cape Peninsula are a self-supporting community. Some can trace their ancestry in the area back over nearly two centuries. The men in this group do not drink and the women do not rule the homes (Whisson and Kaplinsky, 1969). A Coloured man in Kalk Bay told me, "Do you know what God thought of white skin? He thought it only good enough to put on the bottom of the black man's foot!" Perhaps the people of Woodstock will one day feel so positively about the color of their skin.

For the people of Woodstock to develop a truly positive self-image, they must have some political and economic power. In a stratified society such as South Africa, minority groups cannot usurp this power from the overwhelmingly powerful majority groups. But through the use of myth minority groups can develop to the point where they maximize the power they hold. The results of such effort has in many instances led to satisfying life-styles. In the United States, for example, Jews control only a small percentage of the total political power, yet they make very full use of the range of political options open to them. Jews are proud to be Jews because they participate fully in American society while still retaining their ethnic identity. Neither blacks in Watts nor Coloureds in Woodstock have come to the point of maximizing the potential for change within their own communities. The

---

[1] I once asked several Coloureds what they thought of a stereotyped, stylized painting of a black boy with large white teeth eating a watermelon. Not one thought that the picture was racialistic or degrading to nonwhites.

reason for this is that they lack the cohesion, based upon group identity, to achieve what the Jews have achieved in America.[2]

A primary tool for achieving group unity is the myth. That the people of Watts have recognized this fact puts them in a stronger position to achieve cohesion than the people of Woodstock. Social integration is impossible without shared cultural ideals. A unified and powerful social and political organization cannot be created without the element of a shared culture. The culture may be mythical or "false" for the area because it has been imported (such as the British institutions that are used in parts of India, Africa, and Asia), but some shared cultural ideals are a necessary component in the process of social organization. Social integration is the process by which parts of an organization come together to give unity and greater power to the entire body. The aim of black nationalism is to use culture to form a united body of black people, thus producing a greater concentration of power. Meyer Fortes and Evans-Pritchard (1940) have addressed themselves to the importance of myth and symbolism in achieving unity:

> Members of an African society feel their unity and perceive their common interests in symbols, and it is their attachment to these symbols which more than anything else gives their society cohesion and persistence. In the form of myths, fictions, dogmas, ritual, sacred places and persons, these symbols represent the unity and exclusiveness of the groups which respect them. They are regarded, however, not as mere symbols, but as final values in themselves.

Black power can be seen as an embracing by a community of a set of fabricated symbols. These symbols—the entire mystique of soul—are not always looked upon as very real elements in the community, even by those who have imported them. The rationale for the myth of soul is provided by its success: Soul has made people proud to be black and to be a part of a group that was heretofore despised by its own members. Much sociological research has been addressed to how people feel about other people, their prejudices and attitudes. But from the point of view of smooth social functioning, it may be more important to know how people feel about themselves. In America, the building of self-esteem and group cohesion in immigrant groups has most often been based upon a mythical glorification of the fatherland and an attachment to questionable ethnic myths. William Whyte (1943) has written of the Italian-Americans in Boston who had their own kind of Italian power bolstered by the exploits of Mussolini:

> And, if a man wants to forget that he is an Italian, the society around him does not let him forget it. He is marked as an inferior person—like all other Italians. To bolster his own self-respect he must tell himself and tell others that the Italians are a great people, that their culture is second to none, and that their great men are unsurpassed. It is in this connection that Mussolini became important to Cornerville people.

Jomo Kenyatta, Kwame Nkrumah, and Patrice Lumumba have provided the people of Watts with Mussolini-like figures. The reason men like Mussolini, Lumumba, and now Mao Tse-Tung have become popular with Italians, blacks, and,

---

[2] There is the question, of course, to what extent the South African government will allow the Coloureds to develop when they realize the full implications of fostering Coloured nationalism.

recently, with young Chinese in America is because successful Americans are typically white Protestants and thus do not provide adequate identity figures for immigrants. As "Doc" told William Whyte:

> You don't know how it feels to grow up in a district like this. You go to the first grade—Miss O'Rourke. Second grade—Miss Casey. Third grade—Miss Chalmers. Fourth grade—Miss Mooney. And so on. At the fire station it is the same. None of them are Italians. The police lieutenant is an Italian, and there are a couple Italian sergeants, but they have never made an Italian captain in Cornerville. In the settlement houses, none of the people with authority are Italians...
>
> Now you must know that the old-timers here have great respect for schoolteachers and anybody like that. When the Italian boy sees that none of his own people have the good jobs, why should he think he is as good as the Irish or the Yankees? It makes him feel inferior.

In Watts, where the policemen, schoolteachers, firemen, storekeepers and welfare officers are predominantly white, it has become the primary goal of black nationalists to substitute blacks for whites in these roles to overcome the same sense of inferiority that Italians felt when compared with the Irish or the Yankees. The functional response in Italian Boston in 1943 to the closed channels of legitimate self-improvement was for the Italians to gain control of the rackets. Blacks, faced with the same dilemma of a blocked access to the higher rungs of the American social ladder, have improvised by organizing black power groups. The Italians used rackets, the Irish ward politics, and the Jews small business to achieve a place for their groups in American society. Blacks are trying to achieve power for their group by gaining economic and political control of the central cities in America, such as Los Angeles, where they have substantial populations.

Cultural nationalism was used by the Irish, Italians, and Jews as a means toward achieving equality in American life. As recent immigrants, it was easier for these groups to use the old country as a focus than it is for blacks, one of America's two oldest immigrant groups. Blacks, therefore, have had to build a kind of revitalization movement. According to Anthony Wallace (1956), a revitalization movement is a "deliberate, organized, conscious effort by members of a society to construct a more satisfying culture." Wallace writes that the reformulation that accompanies revitalization movements is based on elements and structures already in the system. This would help explain how black power is both a rejection of white ideals while it is a copy of the Protestant Ethic.

Black Americans have a history of involvement in such revitalization movements. In 1913, Noble Drew Ali issued ethnic identity cards and promised that one day the curse of the white man would be lifted from the blacks in a millenarian transformation. Marcus Garvey founded the Universal Negro Improvement Association in 1914, which was messianic in nature, and he attempted to form an African Orthodox Church with a black Jesus. More recently, the Black Muslims have attempted a Moslem religious revival in Watts and in many other black ghettos. The central ideas of the Black Muslim religion are not far different from most of the black power philosophy described earlier. The primary difference is their demand for a separate black nation in the southern United States and their attempt to identify the white man as an infidel.

Black power has in common with the peyotist cults and ghost dances of the American Indian the rejection of white culture. The movement is also similar to the African separatist religious movements in South Africa and in other African countries. These prophetic religious movements are racial reactions designed to maintain specific cultural features of African tribal life while trying to recover some political authority. Black power is, of course, far more sophisticated than most of the revivalistic movements described in works of social anthropologists. However, the movement has the same stated end result of wishing to restore or build the feeling of community that was destroyed by prolonged contact with a more powerful civilization or group.

What is occurring in Watts is the reverse of the kind of social change that is studied in developing nations in which rich traditional cultures are lost as the result of pressures from urbanization, industrialization, and Westernization. Instead of a loss of culture, there has been a birth of culture in Watts. Social change has often been regarded by anthropologists as an evil by-product of culture contact. In Watts we can see a people attempting to build a culture, attempting to remake the image of nonwhite people to what it no doubt was before they came into contact with whites. To do this, blacks need a history. Frantz Fanon (1967) has written of the colonial governments that convinced Africans that they "came to lighten their darkness." The effect consciously sought by colonialism was to drive into the natives' heads the idea that if the settlers were to leave, they would at once fall back into barbarism, degradation, and bestiality. Without a history, neither Africans nor black Americans were in a position to question such assumptions. As Colin Turnbull (1963) has shown, the weakest society is one without a history:

> It is in the past that the tribe finds its present strength, its present cohesion, its present morality. . . . But more important still is that in the past the tribe finds the incentive to work for the future, and to maintain its present integrity. If the past is destroyed, through taught disbelief, or through exposure to scorn or ridicule . . . the result can only be total collapse and chaos.

In search of a national consciousness and in order to construct a national culture, leaders of independent underdeveloped countries—even those thoroughly imbued with Western culture—look to the glories of their past. The Mexicans have looked to the Aztecs, the Nigerians to Benin, not only to achieve national unity by establishing a history but to raise the self-esteem of their people. The people of Watts have established an acting group, a writers' workshop, and schools where African history and languages are taught because, as I have previously quoted Ruth Benedict, "What really binds men together is their culture, the ideas and the standards they have in common."

The current revitalistic movement in Watts appears unusual in that it is a conscious effort to create a culture as a foundation for the gaining of political power. But it is not a unique occurrence: A cultural rebirth in Slovakia and Ireland earlier in this century foreshadowed struggles with stronger oppressors. Such occurrences are not unique even in America. David Riesman (1950) has said, "The only followers left in the United States today are those unorganized and sometimes disorganized unfortunates who have not yet invented their group."

People do, indeed, invent groups. Black Americans have invented an institution-alized means of channeling the *ressentiment* (hostility mingled with attraction) they feel toward whites into constructive community solidarity. Thomas and Znanieci (1958) found among the revolutionary Polish peasants "the general tendency to advance" and "the consciousness of the social power and moral right-eousness of a solidary community." The new leaders in Watts are attempting to create such a revolutionary attitude. How they will direct this attitude once it is achieved will be known only when the time comes. It can be said, however, that the process of changing the attitudes of the people of Watts has created a more stable, more highly organized, and more politically differentiated community than before.

Watts has gone further than Woodstock in solving its own internal political and social problems. The black power solution to the ills of mother-dominated families, low self-esteem, and community political disorganization appears to be working. The attempts among Coloureds to integrate with whites at the expense of building their own community has had the effect of preventing the kind of solution that has come about in Watts.

Simon Rodia was an Italian immigrant who lived in Watts before the area became a black neighborhood. Several multistory towers that he built in Watts with his bare hands have since become the symbol of the black community. The towers are decorated with old soda bottles, seashells, and other jetsam of society in an unusual mosaic style somewhere between *art nouveau* and junk art. The towers were not popular with all of his white neighbors. Rodia said, "Some of the people say what was he doing? Some of the people think I was crazy and some of the people said I *was* going to *do* something." Rodia, an Italian immigrant with a dream, presaged the black migrant's dream. Rodia built a mosaic out of the frus-trations and realizations of his attempt to become an active participant in the American Dream. Blossom Powe, a black migrant who lives in Watts today, has described how blacks are trying to build a satisfying experience from the same kinds of disappointments that Rodia must have felt:

BLACK PHOENIX

And so, each day
Became a nightmare . . .
With no place else to run:
Picket fences falling down,
Sidewalks crumbling on the ground,
Hunger crawling all around . . .
Waiting for tomorrow!
And the Time . . . running swiftly,
Stopped to sift through the ashes
With barely visible picks
And such weak hands—
Crying! Brooding! Trying somehow
To create . . . from dreams archaic . . .
From old edicts and empty places!

And so, each day
Became a nightmare . . .
Torture under the sun:
Picket fences falling down,
Sidewalks crumbling on the ground,
Hunger marching all around . . .
Waiting for tomorrow!
And then Time . . . walking quietly,
Stooped to lift the burnt ashes,
Wondering how it could fix
The broken Bands—
Crying! Brooding! Trying somehow
To create . . . a thing prosaic
From kindling sticks and shoeless laces!

And so, each day
Became a nightmare . . .
But, what is done is done!
Picket fences falling down,
Sidewalks crumbling on the ground,
Hunger running all around . . .
Waiting for tomorrow!
And now, Time . . . crawling slowly,
Starts to sift through the ashes
Of this black kind of Phoenix
With trembling hands—
Crying! Brooding! Trying somehow
To create . . . a new mosaic
From broken bricks and charcoal faces!

Glossary

Afrikaans: The simplified version of Dutch spoken in South Africa by about 60 percent of the white population and by nearly all the Cape Coloureds.

Afrikaner: A descendant of the Dutch-speaking settlers of South Africa. The word means "African," but it is used only in reference to whites. Africans are called Bantus.

Apartheid: Literally, this word means "apart-hood." It is the name given to the legal system of segregation in South Africa.

Baas: The same as "boss" in English. Poor nonwhites use this term when addressing whites in South Africa.

Baaskap: This means "boss-rule," and was the customary system of segregation in South Africa prior to its legalization under *apartheid* beginning in the early 1950s.

Boer: In Dutch, a *boer* is a farmer. The term refers to all Dutch-speaking people in South Africa (who now prefer to be called Afrikaners). The plural is *Boere*.

Braai: A barbecue—as popular in South Africa as it is in the United States.

Dagga: A cannabis drug similar to hashish.

Expressive leader: The family role traditionally directed toward emotional patterning and social relations between family members. This role is normally associated with the mother, the person who usually keeps the household in order, prepares food, and cares for the children.

Instrumental leader: The family role traditionally oriented toward the provision of food, clothing, and shelter. The role is basically economic and is usually played by fathers, who also are expected to contribute to familial management and discipline.

Kaffir: In Arabic, this word means "infidel." In parts of Africa it is synonymous with "nigger."

Khalifa: In Cape Town, these are carnival-like events in which the Moslem faithful perform such acts as bodily mutilation to demonstrate their faith in Allah.

Laager: An encampment within a circle of wagons, a method used by both Boer and American pioneers.

Matrifocal family: A family in which the mother is the principal source of economic, social, and emotional support and from which the father may be frequently or always absent.

Matripotestal: Refers to the embodiment of authority in the mother or the maternal grandmother.

Matrilineal: Pertains to the reckoning of descent through the female line, as in a group descended from a common ancestress.

Platteland: Literally, "the flatlands" in Dutch. It means the country or the provinces—often used to mean "in the sticks."

Pondokkies: Shanties constructed of scrap metal, wood, and other cast-off materials. Coloureds build these dwellings because there is no other housing available for them near Cape Town.

Rand: The monetary unit of South Africa, equivalent to 1.40 U.S. dollars in 1968.

Shebeen: A place where liquor is sold illegally; a speakeasy.

Skollie: A street corner tough; a juvenile delinquent.

References and
recommended reading

Benedict, Ruth, 1934. *Patterns of Culture*. Boston: Houghton Mifflin.
*Billingsley, Andrew, 1968. *Black Families in White America*. Englewood Cliffs, N.J.: Prentice-Hall.
  Black family strengths and weaknesses are described from the black man's point of view. A valuable contrast to *Watts and Woodstock*.
Clark, Kenneth B., 1965. *Dark Ghetto*. New York: Harper & Row.
Cleaver, Eldridge, 1968. *Soul on Ice*. New York: McGraw-Hill.
Cohen, Nathan E., 1967. "The Los Angeles Riot Study," Institute of Government and Public Affairs, University of California at Los Angeles.
Cruse, Harold, 1967. *The Crisis of the Negro Intellectual*. New York: Morrow.
Durkheim, Émile, 1952. *Suicide*. George Simpson (trans.). London: Routledge.
Essien-Udom, E. V., 1964. *Black Nationalism*. New York: Dell.
Fanon, Frantz, 1967. *The Wretched of the Earth*. London: Penguin.
———, 1968. *Black Skin, White Masks*. London: MacGibbon and Kee.
Fortes, M., and E. E. Evans-Pritchard (eds.), 1940. *African Political Systems*. London: Oxford.
Frazier, E. Franklin, 1948. *The Negro Family in the United States*. New York: Citadel.
———, 1962. *Black Bourgeoisie*. New York: Collier.
*Gans, Herbert, 1962. *The Urban Villagers*. New York: Free Press.
  An Italian-American community in Boston is the subject of this study.
*Haley, Alex, 1966. *The Autobiography of Malcolm X*. New York: Grove.
  An articulate and moving expression of the origins of the black power movement.
Halisi, Clyde, and James Mtume (eds.), 1967. *The Quotable Karenga*. Los Angeles: US Organization.
*Hannerz, Ulf, 1969. *Soulside: Inquiries into Ghetto Culture and Community*. New York: Columbia.
  The concept of cultural nationalism is explained in reference to a black neighborhood in Washington, D.C.
Horrell, Muriel, 1959–1967, 7 vols. *A Survey of Race Relations in South Africa*. Johannesburg: South African Institute of Race Relations.
Kardiner, Abram, and Lionel Ovesey, 1962. *Mark of Oppression*. Cleveland: World.
*Liebow, Elliot, 1967. *Tally's Corner*. Boston: Little, Brown.
  An eloquent account of the lives of street corner men in Washington, D.C., with an explanation of the relation between employment difficulties and family instability.

* Recommended.

*Marais, J. S., 1957. *The Cape Coloured People*. Johannesburg: Witwatersrand.
An early history of the Coloured people.

Merton, Robert, 1968. *Social Theory and Social Structure*. New York: Free Press.

*Patterson, Sheila, 1953. *Colour and Culture in South Africa*. London: Routledge.
A study of the social problems of the Cape Coloured people at midcentury.

Rainwater, Lee, 1965. "Crucible of Identity: The Negro Lower-Class Family," in
Talcott Parsons and Kenneth B. Clark, eds., *The Negro American*. Boston:
Beacon Press, pp. 106–204.

Riesman, David, 1950. *The Lonely Crowd*. New Haven: Yale.

Rustin, Bayard, 1970. "The Failure of Black Separatism," *Harper's Magazine*,
January, pp. 25–34.

*Schulberg, Budd (ed.), 1969. *From the Ashes: Voices of Watts*. New York:
Meridian.
A collection of pieces by black poets, essayists, and short story writers who
participated in the Watts Writer's Workshop shortly after the riot.

Scoble, Harry M., 1967. "Negro Politics in Los Angeles: The Quest for Power,"
Institute of Government and Public Affairs, University of California at Los
Angeles.

Shibutani, T., and K. Kwan, 1965. *Ethnic Stratification*. New York: Macmillan.

South Africa, 1937. *Report of the Commission of Inquiry Regarding Cape Coloured
Population*. Pretoria: Government Printer.

South Africa, 1967. *Report of the Commission of Enquiry into Improper Political
Interference and the Political Representation of the Various Population
Groups*. Pretoria: Government Printer.

South African Bureau of Statistics, 1966. *Statistical Year Book*. Pretoria: Government Printer.

Thomas, W. I., and Florian Znanieci, 1958. *The Polish Peasant in Europe and
American*, Vol. II. New York: Dover.

Turnbull, Colin M., 1963. *The Lonely African*. Garden City, New York: Doubleday.

U.S. Bureau of the Census, 1966. *Current Population Reports*, Series P-23, No.
18, "Characteristics of the South and East Los Angeles Areas: November
1965." Washington, D.C.: Government Printing Office.

U.S. Department of Commerce, 1965. "Hard Core Unemployment and Poverty in
Los Angeles." (Prepared by Paul Bullock and Associates, Institute of Indus-
trial Relations, University of California at Los Angeles). Washington, D.C.:
Government Printing Office.

Wallace, Anthony F. C., 1956. "Revitalization Movements," *American Anthropologist*, Vol. 58, pp. 264–281.

Warner, W. Lloyd, and Paul S. Lunt, 1941. *The Social Life of a Modern Community*. New Haven: Yale.

Whisson, M. G., and R. M. Kaplinsky, 1969. *Suspended Sentence*. Johannesburg:
South African Institute of Race Relations.

*Whyte, William Foote, 1943. *Street Corner Society*. Chicago: University of
Chicago.
One of the first community studies utilizing the methods of the urban an-
thropologist.

*Wilson, James Q., 1960. *Negro Politics*. New York: Free Press.
An account of black political life in several large northern cities before the
turbulence of the 1960s.

*Wilson, Monica, and Archie Mafeje, 1963. *Langa*. Cape Town: Oxford.
The lives of Africans in Cape Town are the subject of this anthropological
work. It is interesting for Americans to compare the plight of the African to
that of the Cape Coloured.

* Recommended.